Find Yourself, Give Yourself

Dick Wulf

NAVPRESS ◗

A MINISTRY OF THE NAVIGATORS
P.O. Box 6000, Colorado Springs, CO 80934

The Navigators is an international, evangelical Christian organization. Jesus Christ gave his followers the Great Commission to go and make disciples (Matthew 28:19). The aim of The Navigators is to help fulfill that commission by multiplying laborers for Christ in every nation.

NavPress is the publishing ministry of The Navigators. NavPress publications are tools to help Christians grow. Although publications alone cannot make disciples or change lives, they can help believers learn biblical discipleship and apply what they learn to their lives and ministries.

Printed in the United States of America

To

My parents—who were used by God to prepare me for a ministry of tough love.

My wonderful wife, Jean—who helps me to be complete enough to serve the Lord.

My daughters, Laura, Becky, and Valerie—who love me in spite of my shortcomings, giving me an earthly taste of heavenly love.

And my dog, Dandy—who, with true loyalty, shows me how I ought to walk with God.

CONTENTS

AUTHOR

Dick Wulf is a Christian counselor and a psychotherapist in Colorado Springs, Colorado, where he founded the Christian Growth Center.

He received a B.A. in social work from the University of California at Berkeley, and an M.S.W. from Columbia University in New York City.

Dick and his wife, Jean, who is also a Christian counselor, conduct workshops all around the country on the topics of marriage, family life, and body life within the church.

ACKNOWLEDGMENTS: THANKS TO GOD'S SERVANTS

In the spring of 1980, I was invited by the leaders of the singles ministry of South Evangelical Presbyterian Fellowship in Denver to speak on self-respect at their "Acts 29" retreat. Since this was the way God called me into the ministry of building self-respect, they deserve thankful recognition, especially Pastor John White. For three full years their church staff has been very supportive of me, and I am grateful.

Since everything I do seems rushed, a special thanks goes to Marilyn Erickson for typing above and beyond the call of normal duty. And for preliminary editing and critiquing, as well as being a quiet but certain cheering section, thanks goes to my friend, Dee Backensto.

Thanks also goes to the staff of NavPress, especially to Jon Stine for his editorial expertise.

Finally, I appreciate the patience of my wife, Jean, and the excitement and conviction of my daughters, Valerie, Becky, and Laura.

In God's special way, each of these people was necessary to the task of bringing this message to you. I hope you will thank the Lord with me for their faithful contributions.

We always thank God for all of you, mentioning you in our prayers. We continually remember before our God and Father your work produced by faith, your labor prompted by love, and your endurance inspired by hope in our Lord Jesus Christ. (1 Thessalonians 1:2-3)

PREFACE

It is my hopeful prayer that this book will help to:

Give growing Christians a biblical way to clarify their identity and pursue opportunities for ministry.

Give defeated Christians a boost by redefining their life options.

Greatly increase the number of people actively serving in God's work in this hurting world.

INTRODUCTION:
SPECIAL NOTE TO
THE READER

Do reading and thinking necessarily go together? Let's hope so. May God richly bless you as you read on and begin thinking differently about yourself. But let me caution you that a godly self-respect is impossible without a personal relationship with God. To be godly in the truest sense, we must know God through an encounter with the God-man, Jesus Christ.

When we first truly encounter Jesus, we see ourselves for what we are—sinners. Whether we admit it or not, we are in a pitiful spiritual state—unrighteous rebels, standing before a holy and perfect God. As we move, by the Spirit's power, nearer to the one and only God of the universe, we are met by the Lord Jesus Christ. He meets us on our journey to God, as we stand helplessly facing the invisible barrier of God's holiness.

The Bible clearly states what is so very obvious in our lives: that we are ungodly and sinful. "There is not a righteous man on earth who does what is right and never sins" (Ecclesiastes 7:20). If we have not been deceived by delusions of the ego, then we know that our own righteous acts are woefully inadequate when compared to God's own righteousness. "All our righteous acts are like filthy rags" (Isaiah 64:6).

When we think clearly about ourselves, we have to admit that our motivations are often selfish, not glorifying to God. Our efforts of good works are pitifully inadequate. Thus, the person who can see himself as he is—a sinner who falls short of the purity required for fellowship with an absolutely pure and holy God (Romans 3:23)—will admit that he needs outside help.

Because of God's holiness and our sinfulness, there is a great spiritual separation between God and fallen mankind. Just as oil and water cannot mix, so also a sinner cannot reach God through his own efforts. The result of man's imperfection is eternal separation from God. Jesus himself said, "This is how it will be at the end of the age. The angels will come and separate the wicked from the righteous and throw them into the fiery furnace" (Matthew 13:49-50).

Jesus Christ is the Righteous One who has come to rescue us from our difficult spiritual plight. He is the only possible bridge across the chasm that separates us from God because of our sin. Upon the cross where he died, he paid the necessary price to free all of us from punishment for our sins. The cross shows us God's justice and holiness, for he could not allow our sins to go unpunished. But the cross also demonstrates God's love and mercy, for he saved us from the wrath and punishment we deserve.

Jesus Christ died in our place; he was our *substitute*. "You see, at just the right time, when we were still powerless, Christ died for the ungodly. . . . God demonstrates his own love for us in this: While we were still sinners, Christ died for us" (Romans 5:6,8). Indeed, he died a painful death. But he was victorious over death, coming back to life in order to prove that he is truly our Savior. "He was delivered over to death for our sins and was raised to life for our justification" (Romans 4:25).

God himself came to earth as a man, the God-man Jesus Christ, to live a perfect life and to die in order to provide the perfect sacrifice for our sins. Those people who have a committed faith in his death and resurrection on their behalf have eternal life. They become righteous, having his perfect righteousness put on their account. The apostle Peter tells us, "He himself bore our sins in his body on the tree, so that we might die to sins and live for righteousness; by his wounds you have been healed" (1 Peter 2:24).

Belief and trust in Christ's substitutionary death brings us into fellowship with God, clothing us in Christ's righteousness, and thus enabling us to come into the presence of the living God. Paul describes the logic of this spiritual transition when he says, "Therefore, since we have been justified through faith, we have peace with God through our Lord Jesus Christ, through whom we have gained access by faith into this grace in which we now stand" (Romans 5:1-2).

Your journey to a godly self-respect must begin with a trust in God's plan for your deliverance by the God-man. A counterfeit self-respect would result from any other foundation. Consider carefully the following invitation from God through the writing of the apostle Paul:

> Dear friends . . . This letter is from Paul, Jesus Christ's slave, chosen to be a missionary, and sent out to preach God's Good News. This Good News was promised long ago by God's prophets in the Old Testament. It is the Good News about his Son, Jesus Christ our Lord, who came as a human baby, born into King David's royal family line; and by being raised from the dead he was proved to be the mighty Son of God, with the holy nature of God himself.
>
> And now, through Christ, all the kindness of God has been poured out upon us undeserving sinners; and now he is sending us out around the world to tell all people everywhere the great things God has done for them, so that they, too, will believe and obey him.
>
> And you, dear friends . . . are among those he dearly loves;

you, too, are invited by Jesus Christ to be God's very own—yes, his holy people. (Romans 1:1-7—*The Living Bible*)

In this letter from Paul, God is speaking to you. He calls you by name. If you have never before trusted in the death and resurrection of Jesus Christ to bring you to an eternal relationship with God, then I urge you to consider it now. Your self-identity will not be enhanced until you make amends with God.

Tell him in prayer that you know you need to be delivered and that you accept Jesus Christ as your personal Deliverer, your Savior. You've never really lived until you've experienced deliverance from slavery—the slavery to sin. This kind of spiritual freedom offers you the most profound experience in the entire universe: a personal relationship with God! I call out, along with Paul, to you, asking you to consider this special gift from God.

We are Christ's ambassadors. God is using us to speak to you: we beg you, as though Christ himself were here pleading with you, receive the love he offers you—be reconciled to God. For God took the sinless Christ and poured into him our sins. Then, in exchange, he poured God's goodness into us! (2 Corinthians 5:20-21—*The Living Bible*)

Part One

THE PURPOSE:
BUILDING UP THE BODY

1

CHRISTIANS IN SEARCH OF AN IDENTITY

". . . I will build my church, and the gates of Hades will not overcome it."
Matthew 16:18

In the spiritual drama of the world, a war is being waged—the forces of good against the forces of evil. Jesus Christ described his church as the force which will prevail. In fact, the gates of the spiritual enemy will not be able to hold back the charging army of God. The church is on the offensive.

The primary reason for the power and the ultimate victory of the church lies in God. He cannot be defeated. His people will win the battle because he is the leader. He is the one with the big artillery.

The powerful church described by Jesus would not only be noticed and respected by the world, but it would be challenged by the forces of evil. Such a battle would not be fought with military weapons, but with spiritual weapons, such as love, faith, truth, righteousness—all of them *in action*. This courageous church would be comfortable dwelling near the gates of hell, infiltrating any and all places where evil dwells. Oh, what a glorious vision!

But is this what the world sees when it looks at the church? Is the army of God really so strong and courageous? Some people have concluded that the church is a weakling. Most of us would agree that the institution of the church operates at a very low level of efficiency. What the watching world often sees in the church is a religious form of its own humanistic lifestyle.

Such signs of spiritual weakness are a disgrace, especially when the world should be recognizing us as Christians by the special love we have for one another (John 13:35). Instead, outside observers often see a group of insecure Christians huddling together for protection against the evils of the world. Unfortunately, the world experiences our judgment more often than it experiences our ministry of *salt*—a spice intended to make life more palatable, to make a noticeable difference in the world (Matthew 5:13).

And so we ask, "What has gone wrong?" Without truly answering the question, we jump to the so-called solution of more church programs. I propose a different solution: we need to build within the people of the church a godly self-respect, the kind of self-identity that will bring about the attitude and action of a spiritually militant people. A sense of truly righteous self-respect—both collective and individual—is vitally important if the church is to take its powerful role in the spiritual battle throughout the world.

The work of the church is too critical a matter for its members to evade just because they feel small, useless, and incapable of vital service. We must each be ready to do our own part as assigned by God. In order to do so, we need to make a courageous effort to change our thinking about ourselves—to see ourselves as God's people, without a spirit of fear. We should rather be fortified by a spirit of power, love, and self-discipline (2 Timothy 1:7).

Why does the church suffer from this spiritual malady of insufficient self-respect? Many churches do not respect themselves because they are obsessed with maintaining the status quo. These churches don't reach out to their communities to try to help. Instead they stay in the safety of their own little groups.

The Spiritual Wasteland

When things are always done in the same way, inertia sets in. People get lazy. They don't want to change. They don't really have confidence in themselves that they could do things differently. The church is suffering from such a problem: a lack of positive spiritual identity. When a church has no godly self-respect, it has no power. Certainly spiritually lazy and sinful people have no right to have respect for themselves. But the church should never be such a people! We have been delivered from darkness into the light! We have God and we have each other for our spiritual support.

We're in this together—we do *not* have permission to deny our individual strengths or to fail to recognize our weaknesses. This world we live in is a vast spiritual wasteland, filled with lost people trying to find their way out before the dragons tear them apart, limb by limb. If we are to be capable of rescuing these lost people, then we must be acutely aware of our spiritual identity.

What part can you play in the wasteland of this world we live in? Do you, unlike Don Quixote, have the gift of distinguishing windmills from dragons lying in wait? Do you possess the prophetic gift of guidance through vast expanses of spiritual deserts? Or the helpful gift of caring for others in your search party? Or the exhortative gift of keeping others going when the going gets tough? Or the faithful gift of trusting God for your final deliverance from this spiritual wilderness? Or are you perhaps equipped with the gift of teaching the wasteland survival course?

The wasteland of this world is too dangerous for rash, individual efforts. Alone we would all be defeated. Therefore, we must walk the wasteland together, watching out for each other as we reach out to the ones who are spiritually lost. We're in this together because the task demands it and because the One who sends us out says that it should be this way.

The church needs all kinds of people—*but* each one must have a godly self-image. The church itself is one of God's most powerful instruments for establishing this spiritual perspective of the self. Within the church there exists a symbiotic relationship. The Bible speaks of the spiritually organic connection that exists between Christ (the spiritual Head), the church (his body), and the individual people within the church (the various parts of the body).

> We will in all things grow up into him who is the Head, that is, Christ. From him the whole body, joined and held together by every supporting ligament, grows and builds itself up in love, as each part does its work. (Ephesians 4:15-16)

There is a reciprocal, teamwork kind of harmony here. Paul's metaphor of the human body is a good way of portraying the beautiful relationship between God and his people. But, as in the human body, the body of Christ does not operate at full effectiveness if there are various parts which refuse to accept their integral role in the larger purpose of the organism. Furthermore, when the people of God do not have the strength of godly self-respect, it is as if the body of Christ has become separated from its Head.

God states in his word that we are "fearfully and wonderfully made" (Psalm 139:14). We're called God's "workmanship" (Ephesians 2:10); the word "poem" is derived from the Greek word translated "workmanship" in this verse. You are God's work of art—his poem, not his riddle. When you are able to appreciate yourself for your own godly uniqueness, then you are ready to serve God as he intended you to serve him.

Going Through the Fire to See the Light

What exactly is the self-image we should possess? A definition is in order. I have avoided the term "self-esteem" because of the possible connotation of placing oneself on a pedestal. Instead, I constantly refer to *godly self-respect*. By this I mean a redeemed person's biblical identity put into action—the kind of life we can respect because God respects it. When you as a Christian consider the fact that your life was formed from its beginning by Jesus Christ and that he continues to shape you into his own image, then you can begin to feel good about yourself. It is true that you are not perfect, but you are in the midst of a spiritual growth process toward that end.

Some people say to me, "Sure, it's easy for you to say that. You're a counselor. You've got it all together. You don't have the kinds of problems or rough edges I do. You wouldn't understand what I've been through." Oh, really? I have gone through considerable hostility, insecurity, traumatic experiences, and dire circumstances. My childhood was a battleground from which I emerged with many scars. And yet, by the grace of God, I also learned a lot of valuable lessons about life. It's as if I had to go through the fire of personal hardship in order to see the light of my own identity as defined by God.

Back in the days of my childhood, hostility in my family was so great that I grew up scared of my own shadow. But I learned to fight back, and I did many things for which I am not proud. I treated my parents cruelly and beat up a lot of people. But God was there, even then, in my life. I can see that he was watching over me. I thank God that I can relate to the horror stories of many of my clients because I experienced horror, too.

As my clients relate closely to me, they realize that I don't have it all together and that I struggle with many things. But they know that I'm making it, that I'm trusting God for victory. I constantly see God use my pathetic, messed-up past to help others in the present. For the sake of God's work in this world as he chooses to use me, I am truly grateful for my firsthand knowledge of what real family disharmony looks like.

Although I used to be an angry young man, my unrighteous anger has been converted to righteous anger. I certainly have a long way to go, but Christ has already brought me a long way. Once I lived in a shell of fear, but now I can address crowds of hundreds and enjoy it tremendously. Once I was filled with self-doubt, but now I know that I can give life my best shot, no more and no less. I am finding the creative joy in life of being *me*. It's fun to be myself because it's the way God designed me to be.

The World Needs Salt, Not Sugar

Lack of self-respect in the body of Christ greatly hinders the church's ministry. I have observed that most church members fail to see themselves as God sees them. Without respect for themselves, they avoid the vital ministries they should be fulfilling in the body. The church has many responsibilities, such as reaching out into the fallen world on a rescue mission.

Jesus called his people the *light* and the *salt* of the world. But when a majority of God's people fail to act with a respect for that powerful identity, even those with a healthy, strong self-respect begin to crumble under the weight of overwork, discouragement, disillusionment, and sorrow.

Too many of God's people feel inadequate to do their part of the church's work. They feel that they could never do anything worthwhile, or even mediocre. Too many of them see themselves as the losers of life, thus failing to apply their knowledge of the truth that the Holy Spirit lives within them.

There are a great number of Christians with a real poverty of godly self-respect—people who go on to underachieve in the Lord's work all the days of their earthly existence. They avoid taking on difficult tasks, staying instead with the comfortable jobs, the easy ones, the ones that need to be available for those with even less confidence and fewer abilities. Sometimes these underachievers take up jobs God has assigned to other persons.

Some church members don't even recognize that God has specific assignments for each person, and they will probably never wake up to this fact until jobs go vacant, causing a minor church crisis. People in the church need desperately to respect themselves in a godly way, taking on tasks equal to their design by God.

Satan has done his work well. We know from Scripture that he is a brilliant angel of darkness. He sows the seeds of poor self-confidence, worthlessness, and inadequacy deep into family relationships and childhood development. This infectious sin spreads to each succeeding generation, robbing the church of its power by making its members feel less than they are. People begin to think of themselves as sugar or saccharin instead of *salt*.

Please join in the battle for the Christian mind. Satan wants to keep you down, but you have a much greater power on your side. Begin with yourself, using this book together with your Bible. As you grow in your self-image, you can help others in the body to grow. Any church can continue to build the self-respect of its members, seeing that they get into the ministries where God has called them. Such a church can become powerful—evangelizing and helping the people of the world, as well as taking care of the people within the body.

Don't consider the battle for godly self-respect to be easy. You should know from your own life how difficult it is to think rationally about yourself. It is far easier to tell yourself untrue, negative things about your capabilities. In the same way, it is difficult to get others to see in themselves those positive qualities that are so obvious to you.

But we are to be strong people, not afraid of difficult tasks. We are not to run from Satan, but to stand firm and resist him (James 4:7, 1 Peter 5:9) and to be aware of his schemes (2 Corinthians 2:11, Ephesians 6:11). Our spiritual salt needs to be spread strategically throughout our world. So join in the battle, and seek that wonderful taste of victory! God becomes more and more glorified when his people have godly self-respect in their attitudes and actions with one another and within the world.

Our Battle Is Not With Each Other
It is a daily spiritual tragedy that members of a church feel threatened by the strengths of other Christians. The people who feel uneasy with the strengths of others tend to focus on their own inadequacies. In doing so they fail to recognize the others' needs,

and thus they fail to minister to them with the power, talent, and gifts God has given for that purpose. Furthermore, those who are threatened sometimes become competitive in an effort to deny those other people's strengths, and so they create the illusion of having a greater strength within themselves. This kind of competition can be a disaster for both the individuals and the church body.

Often Christians become blind to the needs of others within the church. When we are confronted with someone who is really good at something, we should rejoice (1 Corinthians 12:25-26), rather than feel bad about ourselves. We do not necessarily need to possess that other person's strength to be worthwhile Christians. Inferior feelings often lead us to focus too much attention on ourselves, thus causing our failure to perceive the needs of others—something which takes a lot of concentration. In such a case, we consequently miss opportunities to help, even in areas where we feel competent.

The blindness of self-centeredness, whatever the reason or cause, is a very great handicap. A word which is the opposite of love is *selfishness*. Selfish or conceited persons are those who are not comfortable with themselves. They are filled with self-hatred, even though some mask it with conceit.

Whenever we're threatened, our perception becomes limited and our focus turns inward. The mind becomes obsessed by concern for self. At the particular point of being threatened by other people, we are hard pressed to put into application our Lord's command to deny self, pick up our cross, and follow him (Mark 8:34). When we focus on ourselves, we fail to see other people's needs. Ironically, this failure often comes about because we feel as if we should be able to do all things for all people. We don't get a grasp of God's plan for the universe, and for our own area and church.

We often forget that God, in his farsighted creativity, has a plan in which various people are being prepared to perform certain assignments *for him*. We sometimes think we should be able to do everything ourselves, even when the Bible tells us, "The Lord has assigned to each his task" (1 Corinthians 3:5). So we get threatened by other people because of their strengths. We say to ourselves, "Well, to be any good, I guess I have to be like that." But that's not true.

We have a tendency to compete when we see someone who has a strength greater than ours. Because of childhood messages that we must be "the very best" or else we are less than worthy, we can become threatened by anyone who can do something better than we can. God gives us strength in certain areas, but he warns us not to worry about whether we're stronger or weaker than someone else with those same abilities.

Can you imagine your right hand fighting with your left hand to grab the fork at mealtime? Can you imagine a winning football team whose players compete with one another instead of with the opposing team? Of course you can't, because it's total nonsense! And yet we don't recognize that kind of nonsense in the church. We tend to compete with each other even though it's spiritual insanity.

But keep in mind that the solution to such nonsense is not condemnation of those with competitive spirits. We have not been given the ministry of judgment—that is reserved for Jesus Christ himself (John 5:22,27). But we have been given the ministry of helping and reconciliation (2 Corinthians 5:17-21). People who do not like themselves and who compete with others within the church need help to develop a godly self-respect. With a strong spiritual self-identity, we can do battle against the striving and competing that weakens the internal, cooperative effort of the church.

Unique People Make a Unique Church
Strangely enough, we often don't want people around us to be special. God placed them there for our benefit, and yet so many of us don't want to recognize the talent in other people. Do you know why that is? It's probably because we have not yet found our own special talents and accepted God's appointed place of service for us.

When we grasp that we were created by God to do something unique—something he wants *us* and not someone else to do—hopefully we will no longer be threatened by other people's strengths. Consider the story of the village girl who had an exceptional ability to hear sounds far away which none of the other villagers could hear. The other villagers didn't consider her unique hearing ability to be an indication that she was special. Instead they thought she was a freak of nature who was "touched of mind." Because the girl wanted to be accepted by the others, she did not develop her gift, but ignored it—she didn't want to be *different*.

This village was located in a land where dragons were lurking about. The villagers had survived a dragon attack once in the distant past through their united efforts. However, the dragon had not returned for many years, and so the people grew weak and competitive. They closed their minds to the reality of dragons. But one day the dragon returned to the village. How unfortunate was the young girl's lack of self-respect, for by the time the sound of dragon flight could be heard by the normal ear, it was too late.

If only the villagers had appreciated the value of the girl's gift. If only they had encouraged her. But they didn't do that. And when they denied that she had something special, the girl ceased to believe in herself. She no longer used her special gift for the benefit of other people.

Too often we do that in the church. We fail to see the unique abilities of our people. We need to get in the habit of taking a look around the church, recognizing and cherishing what each person has for the good of our friends, our families, and ourselves.

Scripture clearly shows that God variously designs and arranges his people in the church, each to do a special part. Without godly self-respect, members of the church will not be able to fulfill this vision. Many godly people do not have a self-respect which motivates them to courageous action in the church. Conversely, many individuals with a worldly self-respect must become godly in order to be used by God in the church.

Godly self-respect enables people to love one another—to love others as themselves (Mark 12:30-31). They can likewise respect others as they respect themselves. Such free and easy loving relationships, without people being threatened by one another, inevitably lead to open communication in the church—a prerequisite to open ministry. Individuals with self-respect feel free to confess their sins so that others in the church can reciprocally help bear those burdens. All of the "one anothers" of Scripture then happen spontaneously as relationships become more important than things, and ministries more important than pleasure.

The symbiotic relationship between the individual Christian and the church is a built-in means for developing self-respect in both of them. The individual Christian should have his life plugged into the life of the church, whereas the church should be cumulatively affected by the lives of its individual members. Through such a symbiosis, self-respect spirals upward.

When each individual, out of righteous self-respect, does his own God-assigned work, the body is built up in loving, mutual ministry to greater heights of self-respect in all its members. This process generates an ever-increasing quality, quantity, efficiency, and effectiveness of service to God in a world with a great number of needs. Imagine what the church could do at maximum capacity!

Therefore, a strong church is a church where each member feels and acts like God's ambassador to the world and his minister to fellow Christians. Such a strong body becomes a powerful force to be reckoned with in the world because it is changing things. So you see, self-respect is not an either-or proposition between attitudes and actions, but a combination of both, resulting in dynamic spiritual results.

God knows what he is doing. He has placed us together in the church purposefully; thus he knows where he wants to use us. As we respect God's wishes for his church, we see that this includes respecting ourselves to the point of self-acceptance. In the same way, we ought to respect the needs of others by serving them.

Dangerous Addictions Within the Body

There are two addictions which seriously cripple the church; I'm not sure which is worse. Unfortunately, many Christians are addicted in both ways. The subsequent loss of godly self-respect should arouse us to break those addictions. It is impossible to live a life that you can respect from a godly perspective while you are addicted to (1) the acquisition of money and (2) the pursuit of pleasure.

Christians are seldom much different from the heathens living in their neighborhoods. Not only do they want the good life, just as their neighbors do, but they define that good life remarkably the same. It is inconsistent for Christians to argue against humanism in the schools when they have perpetuated humanistic philosophy through their daily lives. Who is to say, really, that Christians are not largely responsible for the humanistic trend in our society? Truly Christians are the only creatures alive equipped, through new birth, to show the world the value of a non-humanistic lifestyle.

The problem is pervasive: too many Christians want their church experience above all to be pleasurable. Worship is often defined by the concept of pleasure, rather than pleasure by the concept of worship. Church programs are fashioned to be pleasurable rather than to change lives. Rarely do I see churches do things that would change lives into the image of Christ, perhaps because such programs would be painful. Frequently the programs within the local church are wrapped up in a pleasant package, with a humanistic bow for the pleasure-seeking eye.

I'm not saying that Christians should not have fun, but that we should define enjoyment in the context of what is important to God. Fun should be a spiritual rest, not a churchy occupation or preoccupation. As Christians we should look forward to being together and bearing one another's burdens more than we should look forward to fishing, hunting, skiing, or watching television. We should put far more energy into establishing godly characteristics than we should put into the athletic prowess of our youth or the business success of our adults.

Too many Christians seek employment opportunities which are "self-fulfilling." What happened to the curse of God upon mankind for its self-seeking disobedience? Don't we believe what God told Adam when he kicked him out of the Garden of Eden? But many of us are spoiled—we want jobs that are pleasurable, with short hours and two-day weekends. The reason the Sabbath is generally meaningless as a day of rest is that we've been resting all week long—resting in front of television sets and in our social gatherings.

A Christian with godly self-respect will be content to work at the place of employment given by God. Changes in employment will be made in the context of furthering the cause of God in some way. Considerations of more money and pleasure will consequently be less important in decisions concerning job changes. The importance of employment should be to support one's basic needs and to serve God in a particularly assigned place of work.

Even activities of faith are often done in humanistic fashion or for hedonistic purposes. For example, perhaps we determine to be involved in Bible study solely to help us change into better people. That's too limited. We should study the Bible, moreover, to determine God's will, to see his vision for us, and to be able to worship in depth because we know him better. Let's avoid the kind of Bible study that keeps us out of the action—Bible study which is sought for pleasurable experience, which is actually recreation rather than re-creation.

Americans as a whole, in fact most people of Western society, have gotten so used to comfort that they are usually not interested in anything which is unpleasurable. Let those who don't personally know God continue with such hedonistic lifestyles. But such a distorted form of Christianity should be driven out of the church. It is cutting off our witness—a witness which is so often compromised that it has been largely robbed of its power. This comfortable

Christianity is impeding the process whereby each of us should become more like Jesus Christ through spiritual refinement in this life. This kind of compromise grieves the Holy Spirit who lives inside us, quenching his power.

We Christians should never buy into such compromising lifestyles and philosophies. We should not be so obsessed with comfort, safety, and pleasure that we become completely disinterested in dangerous assignments from God. We must regain a spirit of adventure. Perhaps we should think back to the times in the past when people lived for causes that were important, whether that cause was working to feed one's family, marching against an enemy, or bringing about some necessary social change.

To acquire godly self-respect, Christians in the church as a whole need to fight the knee-jerk desire to accumulate wealth and to spend all our free time in pleasure and recreation. We must battle the urge to pamper ourselves with everything comfortable we can lay our hands on. Instead we must derive our sense of joy, peace, pleasure, and fulfillment from doing our own special part of God's work in the world. The seven steps in Part Two of this book will help you find the role you are to play in God's grand plan.

Paradise Can Wait

Many Christians are trying to live as if this life is supposed to be heaven. But heaven is for later. If God had wanted us to enjoy heaven right away, he would have taken us there directly. But he didn't want that. He wanted us to be purified by the fire of service for him in a different kind of world. What a joy to look at it this way: to say, "I'm still on earth—not because God doesn't want me to go to heaven, but because before I get there he wants to make sure I become more like Christ. Then I can enjoy heaven to a greater degree and be more thankful for my relationship with him."

Heaven is for later. We don't really need to surround ourselves with luxury and all sorts of "things." This is a time for service, a time to feel good about ourselves, to know our strengths and our callings, and to valiantly battle against sin.

I'm reminded of a passage about the lifestyle of the world in the last days.

> There will be terrible times in the last days. People will be lovers of themselves, lovers of money, boastful, proud, abusive, disobedient to their parents, ungrateful, unholy, without love, unforgiving, slanderous, without self-control, brutal, not lovers of the good, treacherous, rash, conceited, lovers of pleasure rather than lovers of God—having a form of godliness but denying its power. (2 Timothy 3:1-5)

Does that sound like America? And what about the church? Should Christians be pursuing comfort and recreational pursuits above the work of God in society? It is my opinion that people are usually so drawn to pleasure because they don't have a godly self-identity.

The fact that we Christians often fail to see ourselves as God's instruments in the world is evident when we pray. We seldom pray, "God, what do *you* want me to do?" God is our Lord. He has the right to call the shots. He's a good Lord. He saved us from being lost in our sin, and now he wants us to do significant things for *him* in this world. God does not want us to seek after pleasure and comfort. He wants us to find our pleasure and self-fulfillment in doing his assignments.

We're called by God to be the light of the world. Some of our assignments have to do with telling people about Jesus Christ and how they can have a personal relationship with God. Too many people accept Jesus Christ for what they can get out of the experience. What they emphasize is heaven.

I don't see it that way. I think that knowing the God of the universe personally is so much better than heaven by itself. When we first believe in God, whether it's in the context of an altar call or a silent prayer, it would be better to say, "I'm going to meet—face-to-face, personally—the God of the universe." It cheapens it to say, "I'm going down the aisle to get into heaven." It is so much more special to know the *Creator* of heaven. Our personal relationship with God should not be overshadowed by the place where we will dwell. "Now this is eternal life: that they may know you, the only true God, and Jesus Christ, whom you have sent" (John 17:3).

But once we know the Creator of the universe, something is asked for in return. That doesn't mean salvation is not a free gift—it is totally free. But it isn't easy street once we are saved, for God wants us to serve him through a refining process. Let me urge you to see yourself differently—with a tough, godly self-confidence. It may be hard and it may hurt. But don't give up—God *is* changing you. If you can read this book and remain comfortable, then you are not closely examining yourself. God's refining process hurts.

I remember a time seven years ago when I had to have an operation. The doctor told me that I needed to have my gallbladder removed, but I put it off for a couple of reasons: I didn't want to ruin my backpacking season and I didn't want to be cut open—it scared me.

About two weeks before the operation, after I had reluctantly accepted its inevitability, I suddenly realized the Lord was reaching down and saying, "Dick, this operation is to show you that I can be in control when you are not." That was important to me. Before that operation I constantly paced the floor. I was difficult to live with because of my anger and anxiety over my situation. God said to me, "I'm going to put you on an operating table and you're going to be *out*. But I will take care of you and show you that I'm not on vacation when you're not conscious, when you're not aware, when you're not in control." From the time of my operation until now, I rarely pace.

It's easier now to turn things over to God. That ordeal was an important step in becoming more like Christ—but it hurt! In fact, that gallbladder operation was the most painful physical experience of my life, and yet I'm very grateful I went through it. My self-respect grew significantly through the lesson God taught me during that time.

Just another warning—heaven is for later. God does not promise heaven here on earth—just that we begin to be citizens of heaven while we're here. At the same time we're called to be sojourners and strangers on earth. We are to accept the status of aliens, walking this earth doing God's work and probably suffering.

Suffering is not something which should rob us of self-respect, but rather it should make us stronger, thus leading to *more* confidence and self-respect. Suffering is actually something we should look upon with optimism. Unfortunately, we live in a day and age when most people want to convert earth into heaven. People pursue things and pleasures, and comfort is a mark of success.

But in certain times of suffering it can become obvious that we are right in the center of God's will, and there's certainly nothing better than that! As citizens of heaven, we should develop a whole different way of seeing life. For example, the best kind of Saturday is not necessarily one that you enjoy on a sailboat, although if you need a rest God might put you on one. On the other hand, your best Saturday might be one of arduous service when you *know* you are in God's will. God doesn't expect us to do what we were not designed to do, *but* he does expect us to do what he has called us to do. Our Creator wants us, in this sense, to help bring to fruition the purpose of our very creation.

Let's do it! Let's turn away from the idolatry of comfort, pleasure, self, and money! Let's move out individually, cooperatively, and boldly into this hurting world. God's assignment to us is to take care of the world and have dominion over it. So let's be determined to feel good about ourselves and confident about our commission.

We need to let God's confidence in us be expressed through us to all the hurting people in our lives who need our help. Let's become so strong that we are *world* Christians—people big enough to take on the whole world for the Lord, not just in the area of evangelism, but also in the area of spreading God's mercy. Let's be all that God made us to be!

Questions for study and discussion

1. Do you feel that you know very much about yourself? Explain.

2. What do you think of the adage, "What you don't know won't hurt you"?

3. Name some things that have helped you to feel good about yourself.

4. What do you hope to get out of this book (or this class)?

5. Do you agree to let the Bible and your Christian friends help you to develop a godly self-respect? Explain.

6. What is your reaction to the author's perception that the church operates at a very low efficiency and effectiveness? Your local church? The universal church?

7. What specific examples around you can you list that fit the description of people lost in a spiritual wasteland?

8. In what way are *you* overly concerned to have heaven on earth?

9. What meaningful things would you like to see your church accomplish?

Note to class leader:
It is a powerful experience when the members of a small group can share their answers with each other. The material in this book can be learned and applied in a dynamic way within the mutual ministry context of the small group.

2

READY TO BE PRUNED

Listen to advice and accept instruction, and in the end you will be wise.
Proverbs 19:20

In God's eyes, *people* are the most important commodity in the whole world, and they are to be handled with care! That being the case, we cannot develop a true godly self-respect unless we respect others. Right relationships with other people are necessary for an honorable self-respect. In fact, righteous self-respect cannot survive in a person who does not treat other people with the dignity a creature designed in the image of God deserves.

So very much in Scripture instructs us concerning how we are to care for others. Respecting others by genuinely helping them cements your godly self-respect—not pride in your *self*, but confidence that God works through you to help others.

Since the treatment of others in a genuinely special way stabilizes our self-respect, it is important to learn how to perform responsibly in our God-assigned roles with others. The Bible provides an excellent guideline for our interactions and relationships with people: "Do nothing out of selfish ambition or vain conceit, but in humility consider others better than yourselves" (Philippians 2:3).

The critical ingredient in Christlike behavior is self-denial. Just as Jesus Christ denied himself, so should we consider others better than ourselves; this should be a guideline for our priorities and behaviors. Our strengths are given for the benefit of others. A godly self-respect requires the priority treatment of others through those strengths. "Therefore, as we have opportunity, let us do good to all people, especially to those who belong to the family of believers" (Galatians 6:10).

God asks his people to have a loving *behavior* toward others, but he also requires a godly *attitude* about people. It is only logical that loving attitudes beget loving behaviors. "Be completely humble and gentle; be patient, bearing with one another in love" (Ephesians 4:2).

Continual dependence on the Holy Spirit is a spiritual necessity. Godly attitudes toward others do not come naturally, but supernaturally! Putting up with others' seemingly sinful or strange behaviors requires some of God's own attributes in us. An appreciation of God's creativity can quell our judgments of the different behaviors of others. Our attitudes toward others will blossom only as we yield to the sanctifying work of the Holy Spirit. "You were washed, you were sanctified, you were justified in the name of the Lord Jesus Christ and by the Spirit of our God" (1 Corinthians 6:11).

The Golden Rule of Human Interaction

The opposite of love is selfishness. Ego-centered philosophies, such as "watching out for 'number one,'" have no place in the kingdom of God. The universe does not find its center in you or me, but in God. Therefore, our actions should take into account what he is doing in the world.

What he is presently doing is *building people*. Thus, the golden rule of human interaction focuses on helping others: "Do not let any unwholesome talk come out of your mouths, but only what is helpful for building others up according to their needs, that it may benefit those who listen" (Ephesians 4:29). Even what you say is to go through the censorship of others' needs.

One of those needs is a godly self-respect. The next chapter deals with how to build the self-respect of others. But people have many other needs as well. As God's ambassador of reconciliation (2 Corinthians 5:17-21), you reach out with God's understanding and his ministry to touch their needs with his love. If you encourage, you build courage. If you confront, you build holiness. If you cook a meal, you build health. If you give financial aid, you build trust in God's provision. If you confess your own sin, you build humility in another by your example. If you share a personal struggle, you build up someone else's ministry. And the list could go on and on.

Unfortunately, many people derive good feelings about themselves by putting other people down. They may look like they are pleased with themselves, but they have neither self-respect nor biblical self-love. On the outside they manifest conceit, but on the inside self-hatred reigns. Such people subconsciously put everyone else down a couple of notches to achieve superiority. To prove to themselves that they are acceptable, they live a lie. Conceited people are truly suffering in their self-deception. They need our love and ministry.

How we treat others—either man's way or God's way—will determine whether we destroy our own godly self-respect or cement it by God's commendation. "For it is not the man who commends himself who is approved, but the man whom the Lord commends" (2 Corinthians 10:18). Righteous self-respect, rooted as it is in God's word and God's ways, causes us to recognize the importance of *people* in God's loving eyes. It does not stem from pious religious practices. God wants something more—something that touches other people.

> You trample on the poor and force him to give you grain. . . .
> You oppress the righteous and take bribes and you deprive the

poor of justice in the courts. Therefore this is what the Lord, the Lord God Almighty, says: . . . I hate, I despise your religious feasts; I cannot stand your assemblies. Even though you bring me burnt offerings and grain offerings, I will not accept them. . . . Away with the noise of your songs! I will not listen to the music of your harps. But let justice roll on like a river, righteousness like a never-failing stream! (Amos 5:11, 12, 16, 21-24)

Which Hats Do You Wear?

God has already assigned "people ministries" to you in the various roles he has given you. Your interpersonal roles—whether child, relative, father, mother, brother, sister, husband, wife, employee, employer, friend, fellow believer, church worker, or minister of God's grace in its various forms (1 Peter 4:10)—define a great deal of your ministry responsibilities to other people. Each of us wears many hats; that is, we represent different things to different people.

So why would we expect God to give us additional, special ministries when we ignore those he has so obviously assigned through the teaching of Scripture? For example, I see so many people struggling to discover God's will for their ministry when they are not really trying to be the kind of husband or wife God wants them to be. Why would God entrust servants like you and me with lots of special revelations of his will for us when we blatantly discount or ignore that great portion of his will that he has clearly spelled out in the Bible?

The first assignment God gave to man (after the arduous task of naming all of the animals) was *taking care of a spouse*. If you are a husband or a wife, your godly self-respect will be either weakened or strengthened according to your level of devotedness in that role. You have been given a heavy responsibility! The institution of marriage was created by God so that people might better meet each other's needs. The basic purpose of marriage is that two people should complement each other, filling in areas of weakness by using personal differences for mutual benefit.

If you approach your marriage in this way, if you meet the needs of your spouse and build him or her up, then you will be able to respect yourself. At night when you lie down to sleep, you will know that you did not tear down the precious person given to you by God, but that you did what was necessary to strengthen both of you.

If your parents are still living, then *you are a son or a daughter* with certain biblical responsibilities. God's command is: "Honor your father and your mother, so that you may live long in the land the Lord your God is giving you" (Exodus 20:12). Thus we are to honor our parents if we are to be godly. To fail to do so is to grieve God so much that he may even shorten our days.

Some parent-child relationships are so damaged that this requirement of honor seems impossible. But remember that what God asks for is that we always treat other people lovingly, whether or not they deserve it. This is a sign of God's presence in a born-again creature—that he can love someone who does not deserve it, just as God does with us.

God asks us to honor and love our parents, not necessarily to enjoy them. Hopefully, by honoring and selflessly loving them, a loving attitude and relationship will occur, even though it may never be to the degree of various other parent-child relationships.

And why do we honor our parents? Because God asks us to. We do not need to resent it if the relationship with our parents is strained, for we seek to honor them primarily for God, and secondarily for their sake. Such a priority does not cheapen or lessen our interactions with our parents. But we can feel good about ourselves only when, with God's absolutely necessary help, we have done what *he* says is right.

Being a parent is difficult. Thus, to respect ourselves as parents we must approach the parenting role in a serious and godly fashion. Raising children to be faithful servants for the Lord is a very difficult task! We are really raising *God's* children, who are on loan to us. The parable of the talents demonstrates that when God assigns a task, he expects growth (Matthew 25:14-30). Parenting is a special kind of role that greatly affects the future of the church. It must be diligently attended to if self-respect is to flourish within the body.

Some people are absentee parents in these days of rampant divorce. Although this unfortunate situation puts a greater strain on godly parenting, it does not eliminate God's instruction. A father two thousand miles away from his children can still call them on Sunday night, immediately thereafter write a letter while they are still on his mind, and then mail it on Monday to be regularly received as a weekly sign of stable love. Such a father can still build a loving relationship from which he can biblically instruct his children.

As *a family relative*, each of us has God-assigned responsibilities that require godliness and respect. "If anyone does not provide for his relatives, and especially for his immediate family, he has denied the faith and is worse than an unbeliever" (1 Timothy 5:8). Strong language from the Lord! To have the resources and yet allow a close relative to lose his house because of unemployment or injury should be unheard of in the society of God's people!

Godly self-respect costs a lot in the way of human interrelationships! A righteous self-respect is no cheap commodity we synthesize at will. It is made only of that strong material produced through the Holy Spirit, deep within the soul of a regenerated man or woman.

Friends to Prune Your Spiritual Fruit
Others can be of immeasurable help in the progress of your own self-respect. First of all, the love and acceptance of close friends can help eliminate incorrect self-perceptions, especially if the behavior of those friends is understanding and accepting, rather than critical and judgmental.

Each of us should develop close friends. I usually recommend that each person have three close friends—people you can call up when you're feeling down and kind of rotten. If you have three close friends, you can usually depend on one of them being available at any given time of need.

Those three friends need to be selflessly loving and accepting, not constantly trying to change you. That doesn't mean they shouldn't try to give you advice concerning your spiritual growth. But those who help you in your efforts to develop a godly self-respect will not become overly critical on unimportant issues. They should not force their way of doing things on you.

When you feel bad about yourself, true friends can give you some input that contradicts the degrading, incorrect thoughts you are having about yourself. If, while at work, you are feeling as if you are not doing a good enough job (because of your own perfectionistic approach to life), they will reassure you that your work is fine. When you are feeling guilty for saying something to a good friend or close relative—something that really needed to be said—then friends who are not tied into those same relationships can give you objective feedback that will free you from crippling guilt. If you are feeling stupid, your friends will point out to you all the intelligent things they have seen you do.

Close friends will reassure you of the truth when you are thinking unrighteous lies about yourself. This kind of encouragement should happen when the friendship has developed to the point at which your friend knows he doesn't have to earn your love because he has already been assured of it. When such mutual trust exists, a friend can say things you do not necessarily want to hear, even things you want to resist. If a friend doesn't need to earn your love, he can speak the truth to you *in love*.

We inevitably change when we have close relationships with other people. It is for this reason that we must risk opening up to others if we are to grow in our self-respect. If friends really care about us, they will not sit in judgment of us. We will be able to open up to them and tell them our feelings.

If we want to grow in our relationships with friends, we need to be ourselves and expose our internal thoughts and feelings, even those that are unrighteous. When we see that our friends accept us in spite of the junk we have inside, then we begin to feel better about ourselves. Even when they critique us, we can see that it is done for our own good. It is as if friends are gardeners who help to prune our spiritual fruit. Thus, true friends spiritually and emotionally bring out the best in us.

Often we interpret the behavior of others through the dirty windows of our lives—those negative experiences, especially from childhood. We often incorrectly perceive the motives of a person whose actions remind us of someone's negative behavior from our past. Perhaps we hear statements incorrectly, adding the wrong meaning to someone's words because of a past experience with our mother or father. We then develop feelings which do not match the real situation, and we become quite difficult to live with.

For this very reason we need friends who are devoted, understanding, and accepting of our irrational thoughts and feelings—friends who can be there in our world to communicate through words and behavior that reality is different from what we pessimistically perceive. Such true comrades can draw new, healthy behaviors and perceptions from us. They can reassure us that it is okay in God's plan to be *different*. As they do this, clouds of personal despair will dissipate in the warmth of their loving confrontations. Self-respect will blossom!

When I was in graduate school, I had a supervisor during my internship who constantly kept asking me about my work, as it was her job to do. Because of a negative association from my past, I continually misperceived my supervisor's message, eventually becoming impossibly defensive. My defensiveness was irrational with regard to reality, but predictable in view of my past experience. Before the time of my internship, no one in authority had ever given me criticism in a *friendly* way.

Fortunately, my supervisor stuck with me and I was forced to learn a new reality. That is what friends can do for you in those times of life when you misinterpret reality. They can lead you from your own darkness into the light.

It is quite natural for each of us to incorrectly interpret the *present* based on our learning from *past* relationships and situations. As children, we interpreted the words and actions of the people who were important to us, ascribing meanings to their behavior, sometimes correctly and sometimes incorrectly. We began this process of interpretation long before we had language. As infants, we interpreted the tone of voice, tenseness of touch, and other non-verbal communication to determine whether or not the world was safe, or if, on the other hand, it required some special action on our part for the sake of our survival.

As we grew older, we continued this investigation of life with its strategic action planning. If we felt secure and had a good self-image, we fared better; we interpreted the laughter of other children at something we said as affirmation. If we felt insecure because of our negative interpretations—whether correct or incorrect—of our *parents'* behavior, then the laughter of the other children was probably interpreted as ridicule.

There is a tendency for us to ascribe false meaning to another's behavior, especially when that person's behavior looks similar to past, negative experiences. When we correctly interpret the behavior of others, things usually run smoothly in our personal relationships. But when we misinterpret, we may withdraw from or strike out at a good friend, with unfortunate results. On the other extreme, if we see positive motives where they do not exist, we may end up granting a trust in a relationship that should not be trusted, setting ourselves up for an emotional hurt by adopting unrealistic expectations of the friendship.

Therefore, it is vitally important to work at interpreting the behavior of others correctly. This takes a lot of effort! But the Lord gave us other people to help in this challenge. By purposefully creating us incomplete, God designed us to be with others. He wants us to break through our destructive misperceptions of others by going through a growth process that depends on the help of friends.

If you feel that someone you consider to be a good friend doesn't like you, discuss it with that person. He will most likely hang in there with you and ask what made you even wonder. If the birthday cake you made is a disaster and you feel quite negative about yourself, your good friends are the ones who will reassure you that, although mistakes happen, they are not a measure of your value. Friends will remind you that they do not require perfection from you before they will like you or consider you highly valuable.

Friends can also help you with your godly self-respect by pointing out areas to which you are blind. There are some personal areas that only you know about yourself. There are a good many other matters that both you and others know about you. (And of course there are certain areas about you that only God knows.) But some areas other people know about you that you don't know about yourself—areas to which you are blind.

Trusted friends can point out strengths you possess that you do not see or appreciate. They can also point out weaknesses you have not yet accepted in a godly fashion and sins you do not see or perhaps are avoiding.

The input and criticism of good friends is extremely valuable. Unfortunately, most of us shy away, or even run away, from criticism. As our godly self-respect grows, however, we will more assertively seek out criticism. Criticism should not automatically rob us of self-respect. Our attitude about critical input can marshal its power for our own good, even when criticism is offered by an enemy!

Criticism: The Mirror in the Eyes of Others

The Bible points out that wise men seek counsel and critical examination of their lives. "Listen to advice and accept instruction, and in the end you will be wise" (Proverbs 19:20). Wisdom comes from examination of the blind spots. Unfortunately, looking at blind spots feels uncomfortable. But it is not dangerous—just the opposite. You are in serious danger when you are *not* willing to confront your blind spots.

Try to avoid thinking that the person who tells you something you do not want to hear is out to destroy you. Generally, people give criticism out of good intentions, even if those good intentions are contaminated by sin. When criticism comes from a good friend, assume good intentions. He could be wrong, but you should not jump to that conclusion right away or you will not get anything out of his counsel.

"Perfume and incense bring joy to the heart, and the pleasantness of one's friend springs from his earnest counsel" (Proverbs 27:9). The attractiveness of your friends should come from the counsel they give you. Counsel, in the biblical sense, is always the truth. Too often you want your friends to tell you what you want to hear—what a good guy you are. But if you want to grow in godly self-respect rather than self-illusion, then you need friends who are willing to offer discerning criticism when it is appropriate.

When someone criticizes us, we should try to remember several things: (1) we always have worth in God's eyes; (2) there is always something we can learn from criticism, whether or not it is valid; and (3) it is good to grow in self-knowledge, even through criticism, for it helps us to serve the Lord more effectively. We should learn everything we can from what others tell us, even if it hurts sometimes.

If you want to grow through criticism, there are two basic ways to respond: questioning and agreement. When you respond with *questions*, ask for specifics. Let the other person know you sincerely want more information, making it clear that you assume he wants to help you.

For example, someone comes up to you at church and says you have done a "crummy job" as a Sunday school teacher. How should you respond? You could say, "I'm actually glad you let me know your opinion because I really want to become more like Christ and improve my ministry for him. Can you tell me what you think I've done wrong?" That's one way to gain specific information through questions.

Another way to question your critic is to paraphrase his ideas. You could say, for example, "You think I'm not doing a very good job, right?" (Be specific if this person told you something specific.) Then he might go on to give you more information, because he can see you are not scared of what he has to say. On the other hand, if he is just being destructive, the pressure is on him to be constructive because of your positive, open attitude.

Another variation of the questioning response is to inquire about consequences. You might respond, "What, in your opinion, are the consequences of my 'crummy job' as a Sunday school teacher?" After his response, you might want to ask for evidence in a non-challenging way. He might tell you that three people have left your class. You can then thank him for his help and privately consider the facts. (For example, perhaps three people have left and none have joined; or maybe twenty have joined.) Whatever the case may be, go on from there determining to be more effective for the *Lord*, not just wanting to please the critical person.

You might also want to seek out more complaints from class members. In a straightforward, nondefensive way, you could say, "By the way, I am very interested in your critical comments about the way I teach the Sunday school class. Don't hesitate at all to come up after class and give me your feedback, whether it's positive or negative. I'd like to have that information so I can improve my teaching and grow spiritually."

You should ask questions in order to gather more information. Why? Because you realize that you are worthwhile and that *you can grow*. Even if somebody is totally hostile toward you, some part of what that person says may be true, and you can certainly profit by knowing it.

Another way to respond to criticism is *agreement*. An agreeing response can immobilize hostile critics, but it will not give you as much information for growth as the questioning method. However, agreeing may be a more comfortable way for you to begin your response, especially if you tend to get uptight when people criticize you. For example, you might agree by saying, "I know that I don't do a perfect job as a Sunday school teacher. In fact, I probably do a bad job at times." Or you can agree with the principle of the statement by saying, "Well, I'm glad you told me that. It's important to do the best you can when you teach Sunday school."

How you react to criticism is a good barometer of how your godly self-respect is progressing. The more you understand yourself as acceptable and worthwhile, and the more you live in tune with God's word and your ministry here on earth, the less often you will be vulnerable to criticism. In other words, the more you get upset inside—fuming, wondering, feeling bad about yourself, dragging yourself over the coals for days—the less godly your self-respect will be. Such reactionary behavior means you are still trying to prove your worth—that you are not satisfied with God's acceptance of you as worthwhile even though you are a sinner.

Let me exhort you to begin to see criticism differently. Realize that you are basically all right the way you are! When people begin to criticize you, don't let it destroy your self-worth. God doesn't see you in any different light just because someone is criticizing you. He accepts you as you are: a sinner forgiven by Christ's loving death on the cross.

As your self-respect grows and you become more secure, you will *want* to seek the counsel and criticism of others. As you grow in your self-confidence and godly self-respect, you will find yourself asking for people's criticism in order to learn from it. It is quite another thing to seek criticism and then say to yourself, "What a no-good, rotten person I am." Instead we should say, "I was thinking about doing this: what do you think?" Here you are recognizing that it's okay to be fallible, to make some mistakes—as long as you are ready and responsible enough to change.

God has given you the gift of friends so that you can ask them how to do things or seek their opinions about your plans. "Plans fail for lack of counsel, but with many advisors they succeed" (Proverbs 15:22). If you continue to seek the counsel and criticism of others, they will give you their straightforward reaction—and then your self-respect will grow.

Accepting a Helping Hand . . . or Foot

Scriptures clearly state that the role of our fellow Christians is to minister to us in all kinds of ways. Sometimes we hold that back—we want to be the strong one; we don't want to have anyone minister to us; we don't want to ask for any help. But we *should* allow others to minister to us across the board—not only in the warmth of affirmation, but also in the toughness of straight advice. Paul tells us, "If someone is caught in a sin, you who are spiritual should restore him gently. But watch yourself, or you also may be tempted. Carry each other's burdens, and in this way you will fulfill the law of Christ" (Galatians 6:1-2).

Isn't it interesting that in carrying another person's burden, we may be gently restoring him from sin? Think about it. But Christian interaction goes in *both* directions. Allowing other people to minister to us is allowing them to be straight with us, to speak the truth to us in love, and allowing them to say, "I think you're wrong." Sometimes people will come to me about a particular issue and say, "Dick, I think you have the wrong idea here." When I consider their point of view, I often change for the better.

Imagine the great benefit you could receive if you were to say to a close friend, "If you see me doing anything you think is un-biblical—not the way Jesus would handle it—would you please tell me, because I need to know about it in order to change it." If your friend takes you seriously and tries to give you godly correction, and if you handle it calmly without defensiveness or self-condemnation, then he will know that you were really serious about your request for feedback and godly correction. Your friend will give you advice because he cares for you and because he *wants* you to be more like Christ.

So you can see how invaluable friends are in your spiritual growth. Sometimes a friend may realize that you need some tough love—perhaps not only a helping *hand,* but also a *foot.* Be meek enough and wise enough to accept both. For wisdom goes hand in hand with humility.

Other Christians are so important in the process of our sanctification that we must beware the danger of the "electronic church." Anyone who is able to attend a church, but instead makes the radio or television his main encounter with the body of Christ, is making a great mistake. A godly life cannot develop in isolation from face-to-face contact with other Christians. Each of us needs brothers and sisters, ministering to us as well as allowing us to minister to them. We need to help each other with all those biblical exhortations so that we can together worship and serve the Lord effectively.

We are being re-created into the image of Jesus Christ! "We, who with unveiled faces all reflect the Lord's glory, are being transformed into his likeness with ever-increasing glory, which comes from the Lord, who is the Spirit" (2 Corinthians 3:18).

God uses other people in the process of your sanctification. Therefore, always try to perceive others as tremendous resources for your growth in Christ. They are resources to help you know more about yourself, to encourage you by standing by you, to pray for you, to teach you, and to walk the road of faith with you. That is God's design for the church—the united strength of God's people living and working together.

Questions for study and discussion

1. What kinds of personal behavior make it difficult for you to love others?

2. After studying Ephesians 4:29, determine what you will need to change in your behavior toward those kinds of people you have trouble loving.

3. Name three close friends with whom you can be fairly honest. (If you do not have three friends you trust, write the names of three people who could become true friends. List some ways you can help each one become your close friend.) List beside their names some ways they could help you improve your self-perceptions.

4. Meditate on Proverbs 19:20. Write down some ways you can apply this verse in your life.

5. As a general rule, how do you handle criticism? What response to criticism would you like to develop?

6. Meditate on Proverbs 15:22. In what areas should you seek godly advice? From whom should you seek this advice?

7. In order for your own godly self-respect to grow, are there any relationship problems with people that you need to resolve that have not yet been addressed in the above questions? If so, list the problems and the best solutions you can think of. If possible, support your solutions with Scripture.

Note to class leader:
The answers to the third and seventh questions should be shared only in close groups where members have clearly demonstrated accepting attitudes. In new groups and groups without close relationships, begin sharing with the fourth, fifth, and sixth questions, proceeding to the first and second if all goes constructively.

3

HELPING OTHERS GROW

Each of us should please his neighbor for his good, to build him up.
Romans 15:2

It is just not enough to focus on building our own godly self-respect. In fact, to do so would be quite self-centered and un-biblical. Christians ought to be in the serious business of building up the self-respect of others. In the words of Paul, "Encourage one another and build each other up" (1 Thessalonians 5:11).

A clear sign of the right kind of self-respect is that we are serving God in a powerful ministry designed by him *just for us*. It logically follows that we should be other-centered, that is, ministry-centered. Helping others discover their own godly identity and develop their own godly self-respect ought to be spiritually natural and rewarding for true believers.

Those of us who have come to a clear knowledge of God want him to be glorified and praised by his creatures. Does it not make sense, then, that we should commit ourselves for the rest of our days to the ministry of helping other Christians become all that God created them to be, so that they might praise and glorify him too? Our sense of godly self-respect ought to free our spirits to accept others who are different from us.

The differences in others should not threaten us, for we should be sure of our place in God's design and covet no other place. By accepting others, we praise the wise God who created them and watched sovereignly over their personality development. Remember the command, "Accept one another, then, just as Christ accepted you, in order to bring praise to God" (Romans 15:7). After you help another person develop his godly self-respect, he will be more accepting of others, thus honoring God with appreciation for each of the Lord's personal designs. We must all work toward praising God with accepting and admiring hearts for everything he has made.

When another Christian takes on a godly view of *himself* because of your help, then he will appreciate and love *God* more fully. That increased love for God will lead to more praise for him through an assertive witness and ministry to people. The following passages demonstrate the fact that God wants us to reach *upward* to him and *outward* to others:

Through Jesus, therefore, let us continually offer to God a sacrifice of praise—the fruit of lips that confess his name. And do not forget to do good and to share with others, for with such sacrifices God is pleased. (Hebrews 13:15-16)

"You are the salt of the earth. But if the salt loses its saltiness, how can it be made salty again? It is no longer good for anything, except to be thrown out and trampled by men.

"You are the light of the world. A city on a hill cannot be hidden. Neither do people light a lamp and put it under a bowl. Instead they put it on its stand, and it gives light to everyone in the house. In the same way, let your light shine before men, that they may see your good deeds and praise your Father in heaven." (Matthew 5:13-16)

This service that you perform is not only supplying the needs of God's people but is also overflowing in many expressions of thanks to God. Because of the service by which you have proved yourselves, men will praise God for the obedience that accompanies your confession of the gospel of Christ, and for your generosity in sharing with them and with everyone else. (2 Corinthians 9:12-13)

Godly people seek to bring glory to God! They try to improve the ability of other Christians to obey him, and in doing so they express genuine praise for the Father. Christians who possess a godly self-respect are able to serve well in this process.

By building up the self-respect of other Christians, you help to build a stronger church. This should be a major goal in your life. For the church as a whole has the breadth to glorify and praise God in much greater ways than individual Christians can. The Bible tells us:

"I will build my church, and the gates of Hades will not overcome it." (Matthew 16:18)

It was [Christ] who gave some to be apostles, some to be prophets, some to be evangelists, and some to be pastors and teachers, to prepare God's people for works of service, so that the body of Christ may be built up until we all reach unity in the faith and in the knowledge of the Son of God and become mature, attaining to the whole measure of the fullness of Christ. (Ephesians 4:11-13)

Now to him who is able to do immeasurably more than all we ask or imagine, according to his power that is at work within us, to him be glory in the church and in Christ Jesus throughout all generations, for ever and ever! Amen. (Ephesians 3:20-21)

Your part in the work of the church includes building the effectiveness of other members, so that a strong army may go out into battle against the evil one. With such collective strength, the church will be mature and unified in the knowledge of God—all that Christ meant the church to be. This is a major biblical goal: strengthening the various parts of Christ's body so that they might have a godly self-respect and thus a readiness to minister in their respective sectors of battle.

Reaching Out With Unconditional Love

Since the source of many people's *self-disrespect* is conditional love from important people in their lives, we can greatly help others to love themselves in a godly fashion by loving them *unconditionally*—without strings attached. We affirm people when we love them unconditionally. In doing so, we are acting in imitation of God, who accepts us and loves us in spite of our sinfulness and our personal flaws.

But to love someone unconditionally is not easy at all! To do so successfully requires a good self-image and a great deal of help from the Lord. Our prayer for power to love unconditionally, in the pattern of God, is vitally important. God alone can provide the ability for us to love in this fully committed way.

A Christian who disrespects himself, who does not appreciate the person God made him to be, has learned to look down on himself as a result of *conditional* love, usually received as a child. Unwise parental decisions regarding right behavior and physical attractiveness sometimes cause a withholding of favor—a signal which children perceive on the powerful non-verbal level. They grow up feeling they are not quite acceptable. As a result, they hold themselves back in many ways from living and working in both the world and the church. What a shame!

Most parents do not intentionally fail in their parental role. Sin is well ingrained, and all too often unconscious. The human race is thoroughly infected with sin. Many parents unknowingly cause their children to have low self-acceptance because they continue to follow a misguided parental standard. I am convinced that most parents love their children as much as they are able—within their conditional circumstances. But, while it is the best they can do in their situation, it is still far too conditional a love. It mars the self-image and the self-confidence of their children, and even of themselves.

When you love people unconditionally, you give them many different messages about themselves. At first they seldom hear the messages of unconditional love, which come from God through your friendship. Although that failure of communication is unfortunate, it is to be expected. After all, we are in a war with the devil, who constantly schemes to undermine God and his work—work which is accomplished in the world through his people. This battle with Satan is something we should wage tenaciously as we march with God to a spiritual victory.

Easy victories are not always ours. We undoubtedly need to continue our unconditional love for our friends over a long period of time. It makes the battle go much easier if other Christians also join in this unconditional love of these people we care about so much. The battle may take a long time, because standards of *conditional* love may be deeply implanted in the self-image of our friends.

There may be a tendency on the part of one of your friends to resist your unconditional love, but hang in there! As the destructive forces swell inside this person you love, it is no time to jump ship—the battle rages! God is working to purify your friend through your tough, unconditional friendship. So do not let your friend drive you off. Communicate that you love him, and make sure your behavior remains godly. Don't give the enemy a foothold. Wage a strong battle! It will not be easy, but a victory for God is worth it!

When you set out to love unconditionally, you will probably find within yourself some seeds of resistance. Satan does not want you to love unconditionally. He has always been in rebellion against God's ways, thinking that his way is superior. Beware those seeds of prejudice and judgment within you. Rid yourself of ignorant, sinful ideas—thoughts and values that do not honor God.

There is no room in a godly person for intolerance of the God-designed areas of other people—race, speech, physical appearance, activities, success, tastes, etc.

Each person is, in a way, equally attractive. Like the many flowers of the field, human beings exist in the great variety of God's creativity. To treat some people differently because they are less attractive by the standards of the world is to insult God, who created them. If a person's skin color brings to your mind disapproving thoughts rather than praise for God's creativity, then get down on your knees and ask sincerely for the mind of Christ.

If someone's material possessions make him appear more impressive in your eyes, realize that you have become blind to true, biblical values. Humble yourself before God, who owns the whole world and yet disdains not the poor. They are very special in his sight. If you value Sunday school teachers more than others in your church, study 1 Corinthians 3:5 and acquire *God's* view of things.

Each time the church meets, you should be ready to unconditionally love people of different skin colors, physical appearances, speech dialects, interests, ideas, political views, material wealth, vocations, etc. Your love for God in this way becomes praise and also builds the unity of the church. Therefore, learn to accept personal differences. Then learn to enjoy them!

My wife loves gladioluses. I do not. I see gladioluses with my childhood eyes, as I think back to when I had to dig them up and replant them. There are other flowers I like much better. But if I can enjoy *difference*, then I can see gladioluses with my wife's eyes, by finding out what she appreciates about them. And so I can come to enjoy a part of God's art that would otherwise be hidden from me. In this way, I am more able to praise God for the beauty of something he made.

Likewise, you can more fully praise God if you learn to see life through the eyes of black, white, and brown people, rich and poor people, blue-collar and white-collar workers, Democrats and Republicans, pretty and weather-worn people, young and old people. Oh, that we might double our praise to God by eliminating prejudice in our lives and nurturing an attitude of acceptance and appreciation of others!

Accepting God as Parent

Since poor self-respect is often linked to early child-parent relationships and perceptions, we can help our friends greatly by encouraging them to place God fully in the position of *Parent*. By accepting God's gift of salvation from our deserved death penalty and the endowment of a personal relationship with the God of the universe, we become adopted into God's family and he becomes our primary Parent. Consider the words of Scripture concerning our *family* relationship and commitment to God:

> Praise be to the God and Father of our Lord Jesus Christ, who has blessed us in the heavenly realms with every spiritual blessing in Christ. For he chose us in him before the creation of the world to be holy and blameless in his sight. In love he predestined us to be adopted as his sons through Jesus Christ, in accordance with his pleasure and will—to the praise of his glorious grace, which he has freely given us in the One he loves. (Ephesians 1:3-6)

> Large crowds were traveling with Jesus, and turning to them he said: "If anyone comes to me and does not hate his father and mother, his wife and children, his brothers and sisters—yes, even his own life—he cannot be my disciple. And anyone who does not carry his cross and follow me cannot be my disciple." (Luke 14:25-27)

The Lord settles for nothing less than *the* primary spot with respect to our parenting. He does not merely become one of our parents—he becomes Parent. As Lord of all—and certainly that involves our lives—God reserves for himself the right to call the shots. That kind of control includes how we see ourselves. Our self-image is to be transformed from the delusion to the reality: from our former, sin-contaminated self-perceptions to the viewpoint of God himself.

Like a double-edged sword, the truth about who you are *in a family relationship with God* cuts away false accusations, as well as false pride. Replacing the perceptions and judgments of your parents, teachers, and others with those of God is vitally important. For when you place God on the throne of your life—in the position of *Father*—your negative self-image should come to an end.

You can help a friend place God fully in the position of Parent by showing him how God's attributes are perfect in all ways. The superiority of God's parenthood will become obvious when your friend recognizes God's omniscience, sovereignty, love, and forgiveness.

You can help your friend further reap the benefits of God's parenthood by encouraging him to develop a close, daily, personal fellowship with the Lord. Through this personal relationship, he will feel God's unconditional love and forgiveness, and so he will gain a new knowledge of self-image. You can enhance your friend's understanding of God's role as primary Parent—the Father—by explaining the significance of steps one and two in Chapters Six and Seven.

Reinterpreting the Past

From the time of early childhood, we all undergo experiences which have both positive and negative effects on our self-respect. We are concerned here particularly with those experiences and messages that make people feel less worthy, able, and acceptable than they are. As God's ambassadors, we can help others by showing them how to reinterpret their past experiences.

Early childhood teaches us many things. In the first few years of your life, you did not have any language, and yet you learned a tremendous number of things nonverbally. You learned about the world and about yourself without even understanding words. For this reason, it is extremely difficult to argue with those early messages, for they were etched in your mind without the interpretation of words attached. When you, as a baby or toddler, grasped the meaning of those stern, parental looks, you learned things deep and difficult to oppose, even if they were lessons later proven incorrect in light of the Bible.

One thing that many children find out very early, unfortunately, is that it is dangerous to learn. Little toddlers love to investigate everything. That's the way they grow, the way they find out about the world. It's a very natural thing for them to independently examine all four legs of a chair or to look through the bookcase at all those neat objects.

So what happens in some families? That little child, with the limited vocabulary of "yes" and "no," comes up, looks at the encyclopedias, and takes one off the shelf. Immediately the encyclopedia is roughly grabbed out of his hands, accompanied by a "No!" a dirty look, or a spanking. The message received is that books are something to be avoided. Books are dangerous. To the child, all he was trying to do was learn. But learning proved to be a dangerous thing.

All of us have a number of similar past experiences which have taught us incorrect messages we still basically believe. We do not question these messages because something inside says they are so true as to be *indisputable*. No matter how self-condemning these incorrect messages might be, we know how to live with them (miserably, of course), and we have emotionally adopted them as truth. We need friends who are not victims of the same trap in order to help us break out of our blind acceptance of incorrect messages, especially messages affecting our self-identity.

Many untrue messages actually come from some strongly *conditional* emotions within the family setting. Some of our friends had parents who did not show them much love. The early message they received was that they are unlovable. Consequently, they became convinced that they are unlovable, because if anyone would be inclined to love them, it would be their parents.

After one has been indoctrinated to this kind of negative self-image in childhood, it is hard for that person to change his attitude about himself, even if he comes to realize that his parents were emotionally handicapped in their ability to love. It is difficult to take on a new, positive self-image, to actually see oneself as *lovable*.

But you can help your friend see reality by reinterpreting the rejection from his parents—by showing him that they loved him as much as emotionally possible for them. Your friend could have been led to incorrect conclusions about the world, others, and himself by sin. But your unconditional love can help to bring great healing to his fractured perspective on life.

Some day while you are having a cup of coffee with a close friend who is depressed, you could encourage him greatly by reassuring him that his value or worth is not dependent on the opinions of others. Advise him to give up that kind of thinking and self-condemnation as incorrect. This kind of encouragement will help your friend more than you will ever know.

Some of your friends' negative messages and incorrect beliefs are so strong because they came from fathers and mothers from whom they desired—unsuccessfully—love and approval. They did all they could (and they are probably still trying) to get their parents to affirm them. But you can help your friends understand that the rejection, the withholding of affirmation, and the criticism came from hurting, sinful, problem-contaminated human beings. In other words, their parents were not perfect. And *they* are not perfect either; but that doesn't mean they are worthless.

Ask your friends to reevaluate the many negative ideas they have about themselves. You might just be a key person in loosening the bonds of a friend's poor self-image. Certainly Jesus wants to liberate all of us from our captivity to incorrect beliefs about ourselves and interpersonal relationships.

Some people demand more of others than others can give.

When a major need of childhood goes unmet, a person can become obsessed in his attempts to fulfill that need. Such a person often spends the rest of his life trying to get enough of whatever he was lacking as a child.

All of us know people who make unreasonable demands on others. They are the people who work hard to be the center of attention. Sometimes they want to possess all of your time. These are probably people whose childhood needs were not dealt with adequately. They were either rejected and received far too little attention, or they were spoiled with so much attention that they never learned how to get along without it. In their present relationships they drive people away—just the opposite of what they hope to do. Showing them this dilemma and working through it in your friendship can be extremely helpful to them.

The Dynamics of Friendly Exhortation
Sometimes a friend may need you to give him a good, swift kick in the seat of the pants, point him in the right direction, and put your arm around his shoulder. This threefold metaphor is a way of explaining *exhortation*, a key method of building another's self-respect. The three phases of exhortation are *rebuking, challenging,* and *encouragement.* When you exhort your friend, you can (a) *rebuke* him for his sin and self-condemnation, (b) *challenge* him to use his strengths in ministry to others, and (c) *encourage* his efforts to serve Christ in a ministry and to accept himself as he is.

Rebuke sounds like such a harsh word. But even though most rebukes are somewhat uncomfortable on the receiving end, they can be delivered with tenderness and concern. The main thing to remember is not to deliver a rebuke out of a judgmental attitude. Remember, when it comes right down to it, you yourself are not very pure in God's sight. Anything less than absolute holiness is inadequate for a totally right relationship with God.

While the earth and the moon are considerably different in size, next to the sun each is dwarfed. Thus are the differences in our righteousness and that of our most unrighteous friend reduced in proportion by the unbounded righteousness of God. When we keep this perspective in mind, rebuking can be done firmly, with tenderness.

A rebuke can be softened by a *challenge* following immediately after. A challenge is a vision specifically for the person being rebuked. When you point ahead to what your friend could be and could do for God, you take the sting away from the rebuke and also stimulate motivation to godly action. When you give a friend such vision or challenge for his life, you lend hope to his previously stagnant situation. If your challenge is based on strengths you see in your friend's life, the outlook for a positive change becomes all the more powerful.

Since a *rebuke* implies turning away from something and a *challenge* implies turning toward something (both being extremely difficult), it only stands to reason that a lot of *encouragement* is necessary to pull all the loose ends together. Encouragement provides the support for the difficult journey from the rebuked behavior to the challenged goal. Few people can make the journey without encouraging support. While a rebuke takes but moments and a challenge only minutes, encouragement costs days and months. But the positive results—the changed life of your friend— should last for a lifetime.

Speaking the Truth in Love
You can bolster the self-respect of your friends by conversing truthfully and openly whenever you are together. As Paul said, "Speaking the truth in love, we will in all things grow up into him who is the Head, that is, Christ" (Ephesians 4:15). When you speak the truth in love, the most important thing is your attitude. A loving attitude will usually produce a loving tone. Deep inside yourself you will know if you are out to build another person up or tear him down.

Tell your friends that they are acceptable just as they are.

When you reassure them, you do not have to talk only about their good points. By recognizing their weak points and their sinfulness *with love* but without judgment, you will show that you truly accept them. Speaking the truth demands that not all that is said is roses.

And your communication should be not only with words. When you tell others of their strengths, ask them to help you with those strengths. The proof of your sincerity will be your request for help. When you tell them of their weaknesses and inabilities in an accepting way, validate your sincerity by offering to help them in those weak areas. When you point out their sins, be ready to pray together for forgiveness. But it is important that you *accept your friends in spite of their behavior.* Accepting the person is different than accepting the behavior. When truth in words is accompanied by truth in actions, the result can be quite life-changing.

Self-Respect Is a Two-Way Street

We can help our friends in the church to grow in godly self-respect by motivating them to take part in church service related to their strengths, abilities, and gifts. Since the bottom line in godly self-respect is involvement in ministry, serving Christ in the work of the church is essential. Be careful to suggest tasks to others that are within their range of abilities, preferably just beyond what their previous ministries have required.

Remember that your friends are growing. Therefore, you can expect more from them this year than last (unless they are due for a year off for rest and recuperation). When you encourage others to step out further in their ministry, be sure to give truthful feedback, especially praise and commendation for their sincere ministry for Christ.

There is probably no better way to solidify the godly self-respect of your friends than to recognize their strengths and God-assigned ministries. A good way to do this is to allow, even *ask*, your friends to minister to you. Everyone wants to be useful to other people. In this sense one receives when he gives. Therefore, allow others the privilege of helping you, especially those you want to build in self-respect. (This is, incidentally, one of the best ways to build godly self-respect in your children.)

Do not beat around the bush with your request for help. Use the powerful word *need*, as in "I need your help." Allow others to minister to you in truly significant areas of your life. Since the Bible recommends the advice of many counselors, request the advice of your friends on how to conduct your life. They will be quite pleased that you asked, and only the less mature will be hurt if you do not take their advice. Those few will need your prayers and your caring, unconditional love.

If you, by the grace of God, help others to increase their self-respect, they will probably, in turn, exhort you to grow in your self-respect. Their own greater self-image will give them a capacity to look out for you because they will feel worthwhile. They will know that God is able to, and wants to, work through them. When your friends perceive that they have something to offer you, your friendship will stimulate the continual development of self-respect in both of you. Consequently, together you will serve God more faithfully and powerfully in your reciprocal ministry.

> From him [Christ] the whole body, joined and held together by every supporting ligament, grows and builds itself up in love, as each part does its work. (Ephesians 4:16)

Questions for study and discussion

1. Meditate on Romans 15:7. What kinds of people do you have trouble accepting? What can you do to genuinely accept those people?

2. How do you feel about living to glorify God? How far have you progressed in making this the aim of your daily actions, especially in human interactions?

3. List your three closest Christian friends and some ways you might help them grow in their godly self-respect.

4. With at least eight Christian friends in mind, complete the following form.

Helping to Build Self-Respect in Others

Let us consider how we may spur one another on toward love and good deeds. (Hebrews 10:24)

FRIEND'S NAME	FRIEND'S STRENGTHS	FRIEND'S WEAKNESSES	WAYS I CAN MINISTER TO (BUILD UP) MY FRIEND

4

SELF-RESPECT: A COMMITMENT TO GOD

Jesus replied, "No one who puts his hand to the plow and looks back is fit for service in the kingdom of God."

Luke 9:62

In this confusing, hedonistic period of Western Civilization, the word "commitment" is an unpopular term. While most people proclaim commitment as a lofty virtue, many would have difficulty showing it to be deeply ingrained in their morals or daily activities. Perhaps commitment is so rare because many people feel they have nothing to which they want to commit themselves.

Imagine a young man who is determined to be a quality shoemaker. He commits himself to this quest. He becomes an apprentice and, because of his commitment, he not only learns well, but continually works to improve the quality of his product. This man goes on to spend fifty years making quality shoes because his commitment is specific. He would not consider lowering the quality of his product to become more wealthy. This ordinary shoemaker is determined, and nothing budges him from that determination. When he meets with other people, he feels confident and good about himself because he is committed, and therefore he is worthwhile.

A deep, ongoing *commitment* to your own self-respect and to the self-respect of others is a spiritual necessity. Such a commitment must be *lifelong* to be successful. (Remember the shoemaker.) You and I each need to make the broad, perpetual resolution to see ourselves as God sees us and to act as he wants us to act. We must establish our perspective about ourselves on his foundation for us, and on our consistency in the pursuit of a godly life.

If, after reading this book, you claim a godly self-respect merely because you have been enlightened, then you will be arriving at a temporary illusion. Such superficial self-respect might be convincing at first because you have more clearly seen yourself. But later on there will be self-doubts, for such is the scheme of Satan to which none of us is immune. When those self-doubts come, you may get discouraged, feeling that what you have read was not quite true because it did not hold firm in your life. Instead of settling for an easy self-respect, realize that you must *commit yourself before God* to develop further and further in a spiritually valuable self-respect.

If, as you read this book, you immediately have a new sense of self-acceptance, it may be a genuine start or it may be just an expression of your wishful thinking. In either case, you will need persistence and determination to develop your self-image further, no matter how complete and rewarding it feels now. Therefore, the following steps to commitment are suggested.

The Cost of Commitment
It is important to begin your commitment by *prayer*, praising God for his truly amazing creativity. Step out in faith, expressing to God that, in his designing of you, he knew what he was doing. Encourage yourself to believe and accept that he has made you special and wonderful beyond your present understanding.

Next, thank the Lord in prayer for his particular creation of you, remembering that to grumble about the way he designed you is to grumble against your Designer (Romans 9:20-21). If you do not *feel* thankful, then offer thankfulness as an act of faith. Our walk with God, as well as our relationship to him, is based on the fact that he is who he is, and that he does what he says he will do (Hebrews 11:1,6). Our walk is not based on our feelings, and, in fact, there are many times when we need to ignore our feelings if we are to walk in faith.

When you pray, ask God humbly for his help. Ask him first for understanding about himself. The more you understand God's attributes, the more you will understand why you are special in so many ways. The attributes of the Creator tell a lot about his creatures.

Next, ask the Lord to help you understand your own good attributes or qualities. Ask him to show you the benefit of your inabilities as well. Request his mighty support in your battle against personal sin. Finally, ask God to prevent you from giving up your spiritual struggle to mature in your self-respect.

As you come to the seven practical steps toward self-respect in Part Two, perhaps it is a good time for you to reflect upon the kind of commitment you want to make. Meditate carefully upon the commitment statements in this chapter. Concentrate on one item each day. After you have fully digested the truth of each of the twelve commitment statements, and after you have prayed for strength to make a true commitment in each case, then sign your initials at the beginning of each statement. Make the decision in your mind that your signature is a prayer of commitment to God and to the Lord Jesus Christ, not merely an exercise in personal growth. Commit yourself to all twelve statements within a period of no longer than a month.

Before you sign each commitment statement, make sure you have a strong desire for the object of that commitment to be a reality in your life. There are many ways to define that strong desire. One way is to wait until you desire it so much that you would give one week's salary to have it as a constant reality from now until death. Or you might wait until you feel a sense of excitement inside. Some of us do not show much excitement on the outside, but we know when it is true inside. Make your commitment something you want to give yourself to for the rest of your life.

If you cannot make the kind of commitment I am talking about at this point in time, it is no disaster. What you read in this book, if it is God's truth, will not be wasted in your life (Isaiah 55:11). Over the next weeks and months, you will probably think of some of the things you have studied, and thus your life will gradually be changed, according to the level of your commitment. There may come a time when you will have that kind of determination and hunger to make deeper commitments.

Likewise, if you make a commitment and then fall on your face, that is not a signal that you cannot renew your commitment. Nor is it to say that your first commitment was counterfeit. Commitment is difficult in our day and age. But both commitment and recommitment can be deep expressions of love for our Savior. As such, recommitments can be truly meaningful experiences in our lives, as well as something very dear to God himself.

It is vitally important to understand that commitment is not some kind of magic, but either the beginning or the renewal of a life-changing process. Godly self-respect should continually grow throughout the many years of our lives. It can grow in two basic ways: (1) through an increase in self-appreciation, or (2) through a decrease in self-depreciation. The most positive approach is to continue to appreciate more and more about ourselves over the years, realizing the extensiveness of God's goodness which has been placed in us for service to others. But we can also grow in the consistency of our self-respect by having fewer and fewer self-doubts, self-condemnations, and self-appointed failures.

Whenever we doubt our worthiness, we can see our doubt as either a failure or a growing point. If we choose to see self-doubt as failure, then we will become defeated, give up the ship, and forsake the journey to mature self-respect. On the other hand, if we recognize that in each period of doubting God is working inside to bring us to a deeper level of self-respect, then, instead of defeat, we will feel challenge, expectation, and excitement.

As you embark upon these twelve commitments and the seven steps of Part Two, consider the fact that as you develop your self-respect in a godly way, you become better equipped to help others and to serve God.

Commitment #1: I will accept myself as I am, just as God does. It is important to face spiritual reality. This first commitment asks you to *accept yourself* at your present level of personhood. Self-acceptance does not imply that you are happy with all parts of your life, but that you accept yourself even in your imperfection. For example, you must accept yourself as a sinner. God does. Self-acceptance is not merely saying, "I'm okay." More correct might be the statement, "I'm okay, even though some of my behavior is not okay. Why?—because God accepts me. Why?—because Christ died for me."

Commitment #2: I will be happy to reflect God's glory as he chooses. This statement is about the commitment to *live for God's glory.* It is based on 2 Corinthians 2:14-17 and 3:18, and it is essentially a pledge of submission to be all that you are *for God,* instead of for yourself. We are called to bring glory to God and to show forth his glory to the world. In a way, this is a statement of unconditional surrender to God, allowing him to call the shots (such as how and where you are to be and to serve).

Commitment #3: I will enjoy walking with my Lord in such a complete way that it matters little the places we visit or the tasks we do together. A relationship with Jesus Christ is a commitment you can look forward to with excitement and pleasant anticipation. When this kind of bond is established in your life, you will recognize that being with the Lord (having a relationship with him) is far more important and precious than what is happening in your life at any particular moment. As you fix your eyes on Jesus ever increasingly, you will experience a sense of partnership in which *he* guides the way.

Commitment #4: I will express my love for Jesus Christ through obedience to him—love in action. God is greatly interested in body language. *Obedience* counts. To the One who loves you more than any other, empty words without obedience are essentially a slap in the face. This commitment is a call to obedience as a way of life—obedience for the Lord's sake rather than for personal gain. It is a commitment to consider obedience primarily as a way of saying to God, "I love you."

Commitment #5: I will be humble and satisfied to live as created and empowered by God. The Lord wants you to have a commitment to *humility* in your relationships with him and with other people. At the same time, you need to respect yourself as *God's person.* This is a commitment to stop comparing yourself with other people. It is a call to honor God, honor others, and honor yourself—all at the same time. In a way, this is just another way of expressing the two greatest commandments (Luke 10:27). God receives the glory when you throw yourself into the joy of seeing him work through you on behalf of a hurting world.

Commitment #6: I will work to eliminate sin in my life. As someone who is involved in a spiritual battle, you need to commit yourself to the conscious, sometimes painful effort toward *the elimination of personal sin.* This is not a commitment to passive battle, but it is a call to arms, a call to battle against the various bastions of selfishness within your own life.

Commitment #7: I will accept, be aware of, and not worry about my weaknesses which are part of God's design for me. None of us is complete. God has given us areas we consider to be weaknesses. You need to *accept that you have weaknesses* and that you can't do all things. You should reject perfectionism in those areas of your life where God has not equipped you for perfection. But it is important for you to be aware of your shortcomings, for then you will be able to accept yourself and experience the freedom of limitation. Do not worry about your weaknesses, for worry is really the sin of not trusting in God's care. Most worry is a denial that God is sovereign. The godly answer to worry is concern. Concern leads to definitive action, including prayer (handing it over to God) and compassionate ministry (receiving from God your own piece of the action).

Commitment #8: I will develop my strengths for the Lord's service. The enhancement of your strengths for God's use is a lifelong pursuit. You are called to *improve your strengths* for God and not for self-enhancement. This may require taking a class or doing some heavy reading. It certainly calls for discovering new strengths and developing them further. It may mean getting people's opinions regarding the use of your strengths. Just as Moses had to give up the security of his rod, tossing it down only to pick it up again as the rod of God (Exodus 4:1-5, 20), so you also need to lay your strengths before the almighty God. Then you need to pick them up again as his tools of common grace to help the people for whom he died and for whom he cares. You need the self-image of God's person with God's assignment to love the world through your strengths!

Commitment #9: I will be content with the place of service assigned to me by the Master. As a servant of God, you need to commit yourself to God's leadership and Christ's lordship. This is a commitment to work toward spiritual contentment. Such contentment may not focus on the work you have to do, since sometimes it is too frustrating for contentment. But you can focus on being content that you are doing *what* the Lord wants you to do, *where* he asks you to do it.

Commitment #10: I will always be ready to take on greater responsibility for the Lord. As you grow spiritually, the Lord may progressively choose more difficult or significant things for you to do. You need to always be ready for greater responsibility and leadership when God so requests. This is a commitment to humility as well as to availability.

Commitment #11: I will discover my spiritual gift and use it for the benefit of the church. This commitment relates to the area of spiritual gifts, which I have not emphasized in this book. If you are unfamiliar with biblical teaching regarding spiritual gifts, then you should do some further studying before you sign this commitment (Romans 12 and 1 Corinthians 12).

Commitment #12: I will praise God for designing me and my life adventure. This commitment is a statement of fact and a natural conclusion to the eleven other commitments.

Yes, commitment is difficult. It is like the struggle of the butterfly breaking out of its cocoon, or that first drop of unfrozen water endeavoring to float downstream, or the rosebud breaking forth into bloom. It is like a new branch emerging from the vine, or a baby's first breath. Like most of life's wonders, it is difficult . . . but beautiful. Oh, the struggle of commitment is certainly well worth it! The process hurts, but our spiritual challenge urges us on to the changed life—the life of a child of God growing into maturity. The process of commitment is worth all of the effort!

For meditation and sharing
Be prepared to share in your class some of your thoughts about the twelve commitment statements in this chapter.

Note to class leader:
The class lesson on this chapter should focus on testimonies of commitment and prayer for one another.

Part Two

THE PLAN:
BUILDING UP THE BELIEVER

5

SEVEN STEPS
TO SELF-RESPECT

Do not conform any longer to the pattern of this world, but be transformed by the renewing of your mind.

Romans 12:2

There is a time to think and a time to act. In Part One we did some thinking about the broad problem. In Part Two we will focus on the specific solution. The first four chapters have given us a general picture of the church—a body in dire need of godly self-respect. Now let's consider the practical, personal steps we can take on an individual basis in order to do something about our dilemma.

These seven basic steps provide a way for us to get closer to God, and at the same time closer to ourselves. In the process we should inevitably gain the kind of godly attitude that will lead to godly action—both of them deserving of respect.

Godliness, Not Mediocrity

As children of God in this world, we need to take part in the process of spiritual growth known as "godliness with contentment" (1 Timothy 6:6). All too often I see people living godly and righteous lives who are also full of self-depreciation and discontent. What a shame! How sad that God's people would prevent themselves from living up to their full, God-given potential.

One of the greatest sins of the world today, however, is *contentment without godliness!* It is quite possible to destroy yourself with an overconfident smile on your face. Many people are content without God. Instead they allow meaningless idols to have meaning in their lives. The three idols of money, pleasure, and possessions cause the subtle disease of contentment without godliness. We figure things are going well for us; we tell ourselves that we must be doing all right in God's sight. And yet our self-deception is inherently exposed by that nagging feeling inside that there's more to life.

No Christian should ever lead a mediocre life or be seen as an ordinary, powerless individual. And yet how many of us look at our Christian life as if it were a drudgery? How many of us are bored with serving God? Is it possible for life with Christ to be a mediocre affair?

How could it possibly be mediocre when God designed us to live for him? All we need to do is get in touch with our God-given design and put it to work. That's what these seven steps are all about.

We need to take a close look at ourselves and determine what areas we need to change. Only when we get really disgusted with ourselves will we attempt to do anything about our spiritual state. So, if you need to get temporarily disgusted with yourself, then do it! This particular study could provide the very steps you need to take in order to leave mediocrity behind you and find a new, fulfilling life of righteous self-respect before you.

An Overview of the Seven Steps
Let's take a brief look at the seven steps. They are not rigidly consecutive, but they do generally build on one another in the order presented. You should try to work on various steps concurrently, giving your concentrated attention to the exercises at the end of each chapter. Remember: this is an investment in *yourself*—for God's glory. It is a noble spiritual task worthy of your commitment.

Here is a brief overview of the seven steps which lead to godly self-respect. Through the course of these steps, you will hopefully be able to see yourself as God sees you, to treat yourself as he wants you to be treated, and to act in a unique way which honors his creativity in your life.

STEP ONE:

You should accept and appreciate yourself because the Creator of the universe was intimately involved in the specific design of who you are. You are a special instrument of God, designed to do his work in the world.

STEP TWO:

You should be engaged in a distinctive, personalized walk with Jesus Christ, your Savior and Lord.

Praying Your Own Way:
You need to be yourself when you talk to God. Don't be shackled to a prayer life which is unnatural for you. Since people are all uniquely designed by God, we all have our own special ways of communicating with him in prayer.

Studying the Bible Your Own Way:
Your study of the Bible needs to fit your individual walk with Christ. Study for results, not merely for activity.

Being Yourself as You Obey God:
There isn't just one way for everyone to show obedience to God. God wants you to walk with him as you are. In doing so, you demonstrate your love for him.

STEP THREE:

You should cherish your God-designed personal strengths and use them for others. You are able to do things others can't do, not because you are better than they are, but because God designed you with different strengths for different ministries. Others need your abilities greatly. God-given abilities are something to feel good about and to use regularly for God's glory.

STEP FOUR:

You should thankfully accept your inabilities and weaknesses, allowing God to work through them. Let other Christians minister to you, helping you in your weak areas. If your inabilities and weaknesses are not sinful, then you should see them as gifts from God, not as spiritual handicaps.

STEP FIVE:

You need to be constantly engaged in a spiritual growth process. This growth occurs as you allow God to shape your personal life through a series of trials, making you even more capable of accomplishing the future assignments he has for you.

STEP SIX:

You should constantly seek practical, personal victories over your sins. You should feel optimistic about yourself, not because you are sinless, but because you are putting up a good battle—a battle which Christ has ultimately won for us. While sin can be discouraging, it should not deprive you of godly self-respect. You need to battle sin with love, prayer, Bible study, and planned behavior, not with discouragement and self-punishment.

STEP SEVEN:

You ought to seek out and fulfill the ministries God has appointed for your life. Every believer is God-equipped for a successful ministry. It is your practical, spiritual challenge to serve God as you were designed to do. Only then will you have a solid basis for self-respect and a purpose for living.

Steps With Which to Run Your Race

Now that you've gotten a glimpse of the seven-step process, take time to consider the words of Paul as he, too, counsels you to grow in spiritual maturity:

> I urge you, brothers, in view of God's mercy, to offer your bodies as living sacrifices, holy and pleasing to God—which is your spiritual worship. Do not conform any longer to the pattern of this world, but be transformed by the renewing of your mind. Then you will be able to test and approve what God's will is—his good, pleasing and perfect will. (Romans 12:1-2)

This spiritual growth process never ends. You are called to be God's person in his world doing his business. Jesus clarified this concept when he said, "It is the Father, living in me, who is doing his work" (John 14:10). When God lives in you, he doesn't want you to be spiritually lazy. He has work for you to do. You will not be able to do that work effectively if you have a negative self-image. Wake up! Become conscious of the very God who lives inside of you, calling you and enabling you to do his will.

Life is far more meaningful when we are natural—when we are being what we should be and doing what we should do. We are God's people in God's world, thus we should minister in the place God has assigned each of us. Such a spiritually responsible life should lead us to godly self-acceptance, godly self-image, godly self-confidence, godly self-identity, godly self-concept—all of which I include in the phrase *godly self-respect*.

The seven steps apply to every Christian. Every Christian is specially designed by God. Every Christian should have a personally unique walk with the Lord. Every Christian has been created with certain strengths for a personal ministry to others. Every Christian should thankfully accept each of his God-designed personal weaknesses and inabilities. Every Christian should grow through the various trials of life. Every Christian should battle resolutely for victory over sin. Every Christian has a God-appointed ministry with various avenues for service. Therefore, every Christian can enter into a special part of God's great plan, and thus acquire a godly self-respect.

And so, as you consider these seven steps, may you run your race within the boundaries of your own unique course, as you and the Lord travel together through this hurting world which needs you both.

Questions for study and discussion

1. Define in your own words what "godliness" means.

2. Study 1 Timothy 4:7-8, and then describe the value of godliness for your own life. Be specific and detailed in your answer.

3. Is it easy or difficult to be content with godliness? (1 Timothy 6:6). Explain.

4. Study 1 Timothy 6:6-10. What conclusions can you draw from this passage?

5. Have you seen the truth of John 14:12 working in your life? Explain.

6

STEP ONE:
CUSTOM-DESIGNED BY GOD

For you created my inmost being; you knit me together in my mother's womb. I praise you because I am fearfully and wonderfully made; your works are wonderful, I know that full well. My frame was not hidden from you when I was made in the secret place. When I was woven together in the depths of the earth, your eyes saw my unformed body. All the days ordained for me were written in your book before one of them came to be.

Psalm 139:13-16

The Bible gives an awesome, almost unbelievable account about you and me, an account which should have a great effect on our lives. Each one of us has been uniquely, individually created by the most skillful, artistic, and imaginative architect of all—the God of the universe. The best science fiction or fantasy ever written does not even come close to the nonfictional account of our creation and design process, as told by the writers of Scripture. David described his creation in Psalm 139. Jeremiah likewise explained, "The word of the Lord came to me, saying, 'Before I formed you in the womb I knew you, before you were born I set you apart; I appointed you as a prophet to the nations'" (Jeremiah 1:4-5).

God revealed to David and Jeremiah that they were designed with excellence and purpose. This message applies to us as well. Before we had material form, God knew us. This is a spiritual reality no human mind can fully understand—yet every human soul needs to reckon with it. Amid all the many complex variables of the universe, God included in his strategy one more variable—you. Your challenge is to coordinate your life with his plan.

Designed With a Purpose

How does this profound, biblical truth become relevant in our lives? Observe from the accounts of David and Jeremiah that even before God designed our being, he appointed us tasks to do. As you were formed in your mother's womb, the minute details of your creation were being governed by chromosomes serving God's purposes. God thus plans out the mission of each of our individual lives. We are designed with a purpose!

This truth is driven home by Paul as he puts into focus the first step we must take in our development of godly self-respect: "We are God's workmanship, created in Christ Jesus to do good works, which God prepared in advance for us to do" (Ephesians 2:10). Here we are called God's *workmanship*, a concept which indicates that we are products of God's creative work. Our word "poem" comes from this word. Each of us is like a poem, for we are results of God's artistic expression.

When we observe that God took such special care in our design, we naturally wonder why. But, before we address this question concerning our design process, we should focus our attention on God's mercy. Although we have rebelled against God, he has given us the opportunity, in Christ Jesus, to be restored to him. Ephesians 2:10 states that we are "created in Christ Jesus." As creatures who have received this second birth, we are made new in Christ, a process which proceeds throughout our lives, transforming us into the very likeness of the God-man, Jesus Christ. "We, who with unveiled faces all reflect the Lord's glory, are being transformed into his likeness with ever-increasing glory, which comes from the Lord, who is the Spirit" (2 Corinthians 3:18).

But why are we created *twice*? One special creation was difficult enough to understand. Two special creative acts of God are rather overwhelming!

Ephesians 2:10 and Jeremiah 1:4-5 provide the answer: *God handles our creation and re-creation with special care because he has work to be done in the world.* And he has chosen to do his work, in large part, through his own people and for his own glory. It is as though God has decided to venture into human history, taking along some assistants. It is a very special privilege to be one of his assistants—to be a part of his family. This privilege involves participation in a loving ministry for God—a certain role he has mapped out for each one of us.

I hope you see the great privilege in all of this. Don't get caught up in the kind of mentality which puts stock in the life of luxury and idleness. Such is not the life for an active follower of the Lord. Oh, to restore the logic of the days when the court jester longed to be a knight rather than the present-day reversal!

While the ultimate origin of our poor self-images and self-degradations is the work of the fallen angel, Satan, the seeds of sin he sowed in the human race continue to be passed on to us through our parents. Because our parents were contaminated by sin as we are, they were unable to love us unconditionally. Their love had strings attached, and at the other end of those strings was their selfishness.

There is nothing we as children could have done to receive total acceptance from our parents. We grew up feeling as if we ought to be something more than we are. While there is always room for self-improvement in sinful creatures, many of those things our parents wanted from us were actually more than God expected of us. As a result of many years of listening to our parents' subtle rejections, we become disappointed in ourselves. The result is that we are all affected somewhat unfavorably in our self-image—from slight self-dissatisfaction in some people to major depression in others.

An Identity From God
The first step we must take in the pursuit of righteous self-respect has something to do with our spiritual identity. We are creatures of God, designed with a purpose. Furthermore, we who believe in God are his children, who are given certain duties to carry out in

his service. Step one is a step of recognition. As we recognize who we are in the eyes of God, we see that we have *value which comes from him.*

In step one there is real freedom from the trap of self-condemnation. We can lay hold of the promise that "there is now no condemnation for those who are in Christ Jesus" (Romans 8:1). Before the fall of man in the Garden of Eden, God was indisputably our Father. While he has always remained the Father of mankind, our parentage became divided at the fall. God expected righteousness from Adam because he was confident that Adam could do what was right (with his help). Earthly parents, in contrast, expect things from their children which are impossible because of the fallen nature of mankind. Perhaps fallen parents have good reason not to have full confidence in their fallen children.

But when Christ died, he offered us freedom and victory over sin. The path was again open for an unbroken child-Father relationship with God. Once again we are able *in Christ Jesus* to feel the positive, unconditional love of God, for even though we were sinners, Christ died for us (Romans 5:6-8). And now, with the mind of Christ (1 Corinthians 2:16), we are equipped to hear God's affirmation and consider ourselves from his viewpoint.

When we fully understand that God is our true Father, we can begin to have freedom from the incorrect, conditional messages and requirements of those who tear down our self-image. This is step one. We can reject people's ideas which conflict with God's perception of us. And we can do this without judging and rejecting those people, and without hostility. Our anger at the sin of our parents' unrighteous goals for our lives can be rechanneled into energy to know God as our true Father and to seek our self-image from his eyes.

Thus we are free to see ourselves as capable individuals, created and designed by God to do his good work in this world. *In Christ Jesus we can stand tall.* We can throw off the shackles of poor self-concepts and march out together in the war between righteousness and unrighteousness—a war that must be fought with valor by God's people.

When you think of step one, there are two verses in particular to remember. I call them the two "three-fives" of ministry. First Corinthians 3:5 states, "The Lord has assigned to each his task," and 2 Corinthians 3:5 states, "Our competence comes from God." Clearly these verses emphasize that we are able to do everything God calls us to do. We are designed to be adequately prepared for God's service.

May the Lord graciously allow us to see ourselves as he sees us. As we look at our lives from that perspective, may we truly feel like God's poem, and may that poetry be set to the music of his Spirit. And may we thus make the most of the adventure God has called us to—each of us living in his own unique way, not separately, but together in one great multitude, spreading the rich inheritance of Jesus Christ to a lost generation.

Questions for study and discussion

1. How do you feel about the fact that God knew you before he created you?

2. God designed you just as he wanted so that you would fit into his plan for your life's service to him. How do you respond to that purposeful design?

3. Study Psalm 139:13-16. What is difficult for you to believe or accept in this passage?

4. How might your heavenly Father and your natural parents disagree about you?

5. Meditate on both 1 Corinthians 3:5 and 2 Corinthians 3:5. What thoughts come to your mind for each of them?

7

STEP TWO:
WALKING FREE WITH
THE ARCHITECT

"Whoever has my commands and obeys them, he is the one who loves me. He who loves me will be loved by my Father, and I too will love him and show myself to him."

John 14:21

Freedom . . . something everybody wants. When we take the second step toward godly self-respect, we learn what it means to be *free* in our own lives. After taking the first step of recognizing that God has a special design for each of us, we are ready for the next challenge.

Step two is exciting. It is a step in your life which can *free* you to be yourself! Paul states, "It is for freedom that Christ has set us free. Stand firm, then, and do not let yourselves be burdened again by a yoke of slavery" (Galatians 5:1). You are free *from sin* and free *to live* out your creation by the guidance and in the presence of the Lord.

Free to Be Yourself
Did you ever want to be someone else? Most of us have that experience too many times. As a toddler, you may want to be that younger infant who seems to be getting all the attention. In grade school, you may want to be the fastest boy or the prettiest girl. As a teenager, you may want to be some popular singing star; in college,

the top student in your class; in early adulthood, the most successful young executive or the best parent on the block.

In middle age, you may want to be younger and physically healthier. As a senior adult, you may long to go back and live your life differently, or you may wish you were some wealthy person, retiring from life in style. Such dreams are commonplace in a fallen world, with our sin-contaminated minds and bodies.

The Bible tells us of great men and women of faith who did no such fantasizing while they were walking closely with God. They were content to be themselves—to be the way God made them for the work he gave them. These people of God are our examples. We should strive toward the same kind of genuine self-acceptance, authenticity of character, and personal surrender to God's sovereign position in our lives. Step two encourages us to walk a relationship path with the Lord without phoniness. God wants us to have a true self-acceptance of who we are in his design and in his plan for success in our lives.

Imagine Jesus on one of his early trips to Jerusalem, walking with Peter and John at his side. But the young, sensitive John happens to be behaving constantly like the impulsive, courageous Peter.

Jesus pulls John aside for a private conference. He looks him in the eyes and says, "John, you are my dear friend. The warmth in your personality is from God; it encourages me greatly in my lonely ministry. I do need bold, courageous leadership from our friend Peter. But from you I need genuine warmth and encouragement. Please don't take away from our relationship *the real you.* You were given this special kind of ministry to me. Don't try to act like Peter, for he has his own special calling. *Be yourself* and serve me in the way only you can."

Put yourself into this story. It is *you* instead of John. Can you feel the disappointment of Jesus when he senses that you are dissatisfied with who you are? Can you feel a great sigh of relief as you realize how important it is to the Lord for you to simply be

yourself? Take a little time right now to meditate on the importance of your own self-concept, both to you and to the Lord.

Remember Nathanael? (John 1:43-51). He was standing under
a fig tree when his excited friend, Philip, found him. Philip ex-
claimed that they had found the Messiah, the Promised One of
Israel. Nathanael's reply is not what we would expect. Bluntly, he
said, "Nazareth! Can anything good come from there?"

Sacrilegious straightforwardness! Is that how we should
classify Nathanael? Certainly he was not trying to act like anyone
else. His initial response to Jesus Christ was quite different from
the personalities of the other disciples. Thus we are forced to conclude that his behavior was characteristic of himself alone. And so
this candid man went with Philip to meet Jesus.

Did Jesus reject Nathanael for his genuinely outspoken
behavior? Hurrah! Praise God, he did not! For Jesus greeted
Nathanael with these words: "Here is a true Israelite, in whom
there is nothing false."

Was Jesus complimenting Nathanael for his doubt? Certainly
that doubt had biblical foundation, for the Messiah was to come
from Bethlehem. It was not yet known to them that Jesus had
moved from Bethlehem to Egypt to Nazareth. But Jesus was not
complimenting Nathanael for his doubt, but for his honesty, for
not being false or phony. It was for his genuineness, acting the way
God designed him to act, with his unique personality flowing forth
naturally.

Walking With Your Architect

Taking the second step to godly self-respect means committing
yourself to the development of your own unique, individual walk
with the Lord. But you must come to him as you are. The Lord
made you a certain way and you are both better off if you live that
way.

It is only after we have had the pleasure of knowing God personally, through the gift of Jesus Christ, that we can begin to

develop our relationship with him. That relationship is often portrayed in various parallels: a son to a father, a brother to a brother, a slave to his master, a soldier to his captain, a subject to his king, a dying man to his savior, a prisoner to his deliverer, and a friend to a friend. Yet in *all* of these roles God has called us to be genuinely ourselves. And when we walk alongside him, it is as if we are getting the privileged counsel of the Architect who designed us.

Many Christians base their relationship with God on prayer and Bible study alone. Daily devotion is the high time of their day. After reading this chapter, I hope you will see why daily devotional time is incomplete communication with God, which will not by itself lead to a sense of self-respect. However, when a full life of *obedience* accompanies your daily devotional time and becomes the major joy of your day, then you should be able to feel good about yourself.

The true key to any relationship is communication. But we must remember that communication is not simply words, but also behavior. God communicates to us essentially by talking with us (in the revelation of the Bible) and by acting on our behalf (in his mercy). We respond in our communication to God by talking to him in thoughts and words (in prayer) and by directing our actions toward him (in our obedience).

God loves us so much that he inspired certain men to put down in writing his primary message to us. The pages of Scripture are filled with his communication of love and wisdom directed to mankind. God likewise shows his love to us in each of his merciful deeds, primarily in the crucifixion of Christ in our place. God continues his mercy toward us in his daily, loving care.

We, in response, talk to God in prayer, communicating our love and devotion in words. When we act in obedience, we further communicate our thankfulness and love to God.

Now let's focus on how we can participate in three major acts of communication between ourselves and God: prayer, Bible study, and obedience. All three of these areas can help you mature in your unique relationship with God. Then you will be able to take your eyes off the spiritual walk of other people and concentrate on your own walk with Jesus Christ.

Praying Your Own Way

Simply stated, prayer is talking with God. The Holy Spirit gives us the ability to communicate spiritually, enabling us to confess our sins and receive God's mercy and forgiveness. We should per-petually communicate to God our intentions to submit more and more of our lives over to his control. And yet each one of us main-tains a personal distinctiveness, even as we yield our lives to *the* most distinctive Being of the universe.

Each of us prays in a different fashion. We should be en-couraged to speak with God in our own unique style—to be gen-uinely ourselves with the Lord, which pleases him because he designed us this way. If we begin to pray in an artificial, sinful way, we ought to become aware of God's scrutiny, the Holy Spirit's con-viction, and the need for our repentance.

The real challenge is to put your particular personality into your conversations with God, into your prayer life. At the end of this chapter is a checklist of many adjectives, all of which can be used either righteously or unrighteously. The challenge will be for you to describe yourself by choosing some of those adjectives. Then you should consider how you can incorporate the righteous side of those personality characteristics into your prayer life.

For example, I am an angry person. I used to vent that anger in subconscious unrighteousness. Occasionally I would even ex-press it in willfully sinful ways. For me there is no way to totally eliminate that anger within me.

But really there is no need to force my anger to go away. I believe God, in his sovereignty, allowed me to be an angry person so that I might become a *righteously angry* member of his army. As such, I've become more serious and outspoken than many others in the church on some specific issues.

Although he may not need many, certainly God wants some angry Christians to speak and act as a prophetic force in the church. God might have said about me, "I need someone who will be angry and aggressive concerning the work of the church—angry enough to speak out without worrying about what people think." In light of Amos 5:15 ("Hate evil") and Ephesians 4:26 ("Be angry but do not sin"—*Revised Standard Version*), there is biblical support for *righteous* anger in my life.

As an angry person, I pray in a different fashion than others. I used to feel quite discouraged about this because I was not so eloquent or tactful in my prayers. I would hear Christians praying with a tender spirit, and then I would condemn myself.

I know of people who get up in the morning with sweet praise on their lips. Although eventually such praise comes to me also, it does not come until I pour out my serious concerns to God. When I awake, I usually ask the Lord right away what he and I are going to be doing together during the day. Then, after some serious thought about those events and battles, I begin to consider God himself—how great he really is and how I will constantly need him during the day. This is when the praise begins to flow. Such an approach to prayer is quite acceptable to God—as long as it is a *natural* expression of one who has been created with that unique kind of temperament.

What about you? What are your main personality characteristics? How do they fit into prayer? If you are jealous, can you turn that quality into jealous concern for the faithfulness of God's people? Perhaps your jealousy can be used righteously in your prayers as you appeal to God for those who flirt with the world or for those who place things or people higher than God.

If you are tender and kind, your prayers should reflect compassion and understanding for those people the Holy Spirit brings to your mind. If you are verbally creative, your prayers may be like poems—works of art which glorify the One who made you to be creative.

The main point about prayer is this: you should work at being *genuine* when you express yourself in prayer. You need to take your eyes off the "great praying saints." Incorporate some of their character into your life; it will probably fit. But be careful that self-criticism does not come in and take the joy out of your prayer.

And make sure that your prayers are dialogues, rather than monologues. Prayer is not a form of spiritual dictation, but a two-way conference with your personal, omniscient Advisor.

Studying the Bible Your Own Way

Do you truly want to communicate with God? Then take the time to listen to what he has to say. The Bible is a vital key in our communication with God. When you study the Bible, you are listening to God's message to us, written in the revelation of Scripture. As with prayer, there are different ways to study the Bible. You must find the kind of Bible study which fits the person God made you to be.

It is a great act of love that God communicated to us through the written word. We don't have to hear voices or base our lives on oracular revelations. God loved us enough to make sure it was written down. "For prophecy never had its origin in the will of man, but men spoke from God as they were carried along by the Holy Spirit" (2 Peter 1:21).

To some people, five minutes in the word of God is probably a very beneficial spiritual experience. But just five minutes of Bible study is for me a very frustrating experience, for I cannot read one passage of Scripture without having several different thoughts. But it is certainly acceptable for others to spend short periods of time in the Bible if it gives them some spiritual satisfaction.

It is obvious to me why I need a longer time in the Scripture than most people do. My personality characteristics of slow reading and fast mind for practicality, which have developed under the watchful eye of a sovereign God, keep me in the Bible for at least an hour or two at a time. This is just one example of how a unique design by a creative God can affect Bible study.

My wife and I have had a problem joining together in both Bible study and prayer. You see, I have an analytical mind. For example, I enjoy puzzles, and I also like to invent Christian table games which teach challenging concepts and stimulate spiritual growth. But my wife has the kind of beautiful faith which accepts scriptural truth with an easy sincerity.

Often when we used to study the Bible together, I would find more in a passage than Jean would, and so she would become frustrated and feel inferior. But in prayer with Jean it was just the opposite: I was often at a loss for words and felt inferior. At first her uneasiness in Bible study and mine in prayer were subconscious. Thus it was some time before we recognized why we avoided joint Bible study and prayer. You see, we had not yet accepted the fact that we were different. But now we see that God gave us to each other largely because of our differences.

When God created Adam, he created him to be incomplete even in his perfection. And so when God created a helper for him, Eve was made to be different from Adam so that they might enjoy a mutual ministry to each other. Therefore, the differences in a marriage are perhaps even more critical than the similarities. The differences in a marriage should be a significant reason for your praise of God's creativity and your thankfulness for your mate.

The manner in which we study the Scriptures is important. We bring to our understanding of Scripture our own personality characteristics, values, mental abilities, and past life circumstances. We interpret Scripture and apply it to our lives under the guidance of God, who takes each person's unique being into consideration.

The important point is this: do not compare your Bible study with that of other people—except for the purpose of becoming more effective and devout. Continually resist the temptation to feel negative about yourself just because you do not see in Scripture what others see. Because the mind of Christ is working together with your own personality, you'll see unique things that others will not see.

The mind of Christ is no simple thing. None of us can encompass the whole mind of the living God. We can each understand only a small portion of it, and that portion comes to us in the context of our unique strengths and life circumstances. We are given our own particular discoveries to share with others as we join with them in mutual ministry. Paul sheds some light on this subject:

> We proclaim him [Christ], admonishing and teaching everyone with all wisdom, so that we may present everyone perfect in Christ. To this end I labor, struggling with all his energy, which so powerfully works in me. (Colossians 1:28-29)

Immediately Paul goes on to add:

> My purpose is that they may be encouraged in heart and united in love, so that they may have the full riches of complete understanding, in order that they may know the mystery of God, namely, Christ, in whom are hidden all the treasures of wisdom and knowledge. (Colossians 2:2-3)

Paul then goes on to emphasize again our ministry to one another in the sharing of Scripture, each from his own perspective, for we are differently designed and guided by our creative God.

> Let the peace of Christ rule in your hearts, since as members of one body you were called to peace. And be thankful. Let the word of Christ dwell in you richly as you teach and admonish one another with all wisdom, and as you sing psalms, hymns and spiritual songs with gratitude in your hearts to God. And whatever you do, whether in word or deed, do it all in the name of the Lord Jesus, giving thanks to God the Father through him. (Colossians 3:15-17)

Consider not only your *own* benefit from your scriptural insights, however simple or profound, but also the necessity of sharing your unique perceptions with the church. In the body of Christ we are to grow together. We are indispensable to each other.

Your contribution is unique and of significant value to the growth of the church. My wife's simple acceptance of the truth of Scripture is critical to complete my individual walk with God. And yet, at the same time, my analytical understanding of Scripture is critical to Jean's unique walk with the Lord.

Therefore, as you listen to God, do so with all of your unique being. Pay attention to what he is saying. Carefully and readily accept his teaching, but let it sink into your own personality and apply it to your own experiences. Allow it to change your life as you develop a meaningful, loving conversation between God and yourself.

In your temple-body (1 Corinthians 6:19), let the Holy Spirit do his work of integrating the word of God into your particular life. And then be ready to share yourself—complete with the integration of God's word—with your brothers and sisters in Christ every time you join together. God has something profound to say to them through you—a biblical message which can come through you alone.

To Obey God Is To Love Him

What is the most important form of communication from man to God? Obedience. Jesus tells us, "Whoever has my commands and obeys them, he is the one who loves me. He who loves me will be loved by my Father, and I too will love him and show myself to him" (John 14:21). Here we see that our obedience is received by God as an expression of our love for him. Our obedient actions have more weight than our words as expressions of our love to God.

Obedience is a vital form of communication, especially as an expression of love to God. God is more interested in our body language than in our verbal language. Let's not fool ourselves: we can't avoid communication. In fact, we communicate with God all day long. Every moment of our lives is either a righteous message of our love for the living God or an unrighteous statement of our indifference to him.

God is more concerned with our loving behavior than with our empty words. We are God's instruments to do what he wants done in this world. It is a great privilege to stick our necks out for the Lord, to see ourselves as his warriors, going out to face difficult tasks.

The fact that actions are more important than words, that the expression of sincerely righteous behavior is more important than the empty tribute of hypocritical words, is shown clearly in Jesus' parable of the response of two sons to their father's request for help in the fields.

> "What do you think? There was a man who had two sons. He went to the first and said, 'Son, go and work today in the vineyard.'
>
> "'I will not,' he answered, but later he changed his mind and went.
>
> "Then the father went to the other son and said the same thing. He answered, 'I will, sir,' but he did not go.
>
> "Which of the two did what his father wanted?"
>
> "The first," they answered.
>
> Jesus said to them, "I tell you the truth, the tax collectors and the prostitutes are entering the kingdom of God ahead of you." (Matthew 21:28-31)

Convincing, isn't it? Despite his initial unwillingness, the son's act of obedience was an expression of love. In fact, righteous action despite lack of enthusiasm ("I don't want to, but I will") is a significant statement of your love to God. In such a case you are clearly doing it for him, without any selfish motives (unless you are foolishly bargaining with God that your obedience will pressure him into blessing you).

Of course, there is a more excellent way of obedience. You should realize that whatever God asks you to do is truly the best course he has for you at that moment. Then you can respond immediately with full acceptance that God knows what is right for your life. You can thankfully and joyfully move forward in obedience, expressing not only love, but a oneness with God. This kind of obedience is an intimate expression of your love for the God who loves you.

Why should we show obedient love for God? To earn our way to heaven? No! Such motivation is shallow and humanistic. There is no way we can be good enough to be united to a holy God.

Our *faith* in what Christ did for us when he died and was resurrected brings us into a relationship with God. God took care of a profound problem for us that we ourselves were helpless to do anything about. As one tiny drop of poison ruins a whole glass of water and would kill you or me, so one tiny drop of sin keeps us from God, who is absolutely holy and without sin. But God, in his goodness and mercy, came to earth and gave himself for us, providing an antidote to the poison.

Therefore, it is out of thanksgiving and gratitude for what God has done for us that we go out into the world obediently to serve him. In joyful, appreciative love, we want to tackle the great big problems of the world, helping people wherever we are. We want to be Good Samaritans on the loneliest of roads in order to say, "Thanks, Lord, for what you've done for us."

Thus, as Christians we do not do good works to make our way into heaven. Rather, we obey and do what is right to express our love for God, which is based on his great love for us. And through this process we inevitably develop a continually deeper relationship of love with him.

Doesn't it stand to reason, then—since obedience is so critically important—that you should obey the Lord with your very unique, God-given self? If the Creator asks you to sing, then he wants to hear the beautiful sounds he designed you to make.

For we are God's workmanship, created in Christ Jesus to do good works, which God prepared in advance for us to do. (Ephesians 2:10)

Seeing Yourself Through the Eyes of God

Each of us has different tasks to do and different ways of doing them. God asks for an obedience which is in harmony with the strengths he has placed in us. His power works through the unique design he has given to each individual person.

Whenever we obey God, we need to express a love that is dependent on him. In each act of obedience, we need his power to sustain us. Each of us has a confident kind of love (in the area of our strengths) as well as a more vulnerable kind of love (in the area of our weaknesses), both of them stemming from the same God. We all express love at different degrees of conscious and subconscious trust. Each act of obedience requires a slightly different mixture of these two areas of dependence on God, in response to God's unique requests in our lives.

Perhaps your strength can enhance my weakness, and vice versa. This is God's design for the body of the church. We've become much too independent of one another, and thus our differences do not complement each other in our daily ministries. Our autonomy blinds us to the value of our strengths to others and the value of others' abilities for our own weaknesses. What a shame! For in acting so independently, we are robbing God's people of the full extent of his grace, which works through the coordination of the strengths and weaknesses of his many children.

If you want to use your unique strengths in obedience to God, join a team of Christians who are moving out boldly into this dangerous world we live in. Risk yourself for Christ. You will not lose your individuality. Rather you will gain a sense of oneness as you are immersed in the life and work of the living spiritual body of the Lord.

I would encourage you to value your own unique style of obedience. It is time to stop comparing yourself with other people, and to look to the God you serve. Your own style of obedience was designed by the Creator who makes the assignments! And so you need to look at yourself through the eyes of God.

Think of the individual ministries of the two prophets Jeremiah and Hosea, each living and working for the Lord in his own way. Jeremiah's task was to urge the Hebrews of the nation of Judah to surrender to their enemies. Although it was such an unpopular task, Jeremiah had to serve God by repeatedly proclaiming this message for forty years. Such a major task of obedience required a very special personality. It required stubbornness, hardheadedness, and righteous anger to confront such a rebellious nation. It took great physical stamina to spend all those years in prison. Moreover, it required *spiritual* stamina and tremendous self-acceptance to keep from being destroyed by the unanimous condemnation by God's people.

Next consider the sad story of Hosea, who was called by God to marry a prostitute and to suffer her disobedience time and again. Such a life of personal tragedy gave Hosea a unique insight. The unfaithfulness of his wife gave him an ability to understand what, in the larger theater of life, the Israelites were doing to God through their unfaithful worship of idols. Hosea's demanding task required different personal characteristics than did the task of his fellow prophet Jeremiah. Because of his difficult circumstances, Hosea needed a very tender and humble spirit.

Hosea's ability to cope with intimate rejection by an unfaithful wife was quite different from Jeremiah's need to deal with vehement rejection by a rebellious nation. Whereas Jeremiah's imprisonment required great physical endurance, think of the tremendous emotional endurance Hosea needed! Here we see two very different prophets with two very different messages, given two very distinct tasks because of their very different, God-designed strengths—each of them created by the very same God! Paul expressed this kind of variety-within-unity of God's people in the church:

> There are different kinds of gifts, but the same Spirit. There are different kinds of service, but the same Lord. There are different

kinds of working, but the same God works all of them in all men. (1 Corinthians 12:4-6)

You must serve God in *your* own unique way. For it is a spiritual fact that Jesus Christ has set you free to be yourself. This is the second step to godly self-respect. Our freedom is not cheap, and sometimes it leads to trying circumstances, as in the cases of Jeremiah and Hosea. Each of us faces a different challenge—one that is ultimately determined by God. If we can truly be ourselves as we serve God, then we can experience the positive self-respect that comes by his grace alone.

We all need to establish stronger communication with God. This communication process requires our devoted participation. We need to talk sincerely with God on a regular basis (prayer), to listen to his message to us (Bible study), and to show our love for him by following his guidance (obedience). God has assigned each of us certain tasks to do, and he alone enables us to do them. As we truly serve him, he says to each of us, in full recognition of our own styles, "Well done, good and faithful servant!" (Matthew 25:21).

For meditation and discussion

You can have your own unique approach to prayer, Bible study, and obedience. The importance of being yourself with God—relating to him as you are—is a critical step to godly self-respect. Thus the exercises which follow are vitally important for you.

1. On the work sheet at the end of this chapter, entitled "My God-Given Characteristics," circle all the words that describe you. Then put a star by the fifteen words that *best* describe you. If you think of other, more descriptive words, feel free to substitute them. In this second step of developing a godly self-respect, you need to consider how to use these characteristics in a righteous way in your own walk with God.

2. The work sheet entitled "Communication: The Key to a Personal Relationship With God" is for making decisions about *your* relationship with God. After you have identified fifteen characteristics which describe your personality, you can begin the process of integrating your personality together with your communication with God. There are three basic ways you communicate with God: prayer, Bible study, and obedience. In each of these areas you can incorporate your own personality.

This process of application will not be easy at first. It requires prayer, meditation, and thoughtful application. Please do not get discouraged during this step. All that is required right now is that you begin the process of integrating your personality into your relationship with God. This will help you to take your eyes off others' relationships with the Lord and place them more appropriately on your own walk with Jesus Christ. You will find, over the next few months, that you can incorporate your personality more and more into your prayer life, your Bible study, and the manner in which you obey God. Right now just try to lay a good foundation.

Section on Prayer

After reading Psalm 62:8 and asking for the Lord's guidance in this exercise, write *When* you feel it is most appropriate for you to pray. For example, you might write down that you want to pray early in the morning for about fifteen minutes as a part of a daily quiet time, but you might also decide that whenever you are having trouble going to sleep or whenever you wake up in the middle of the night, you will get up and pray for an extended period of time.

You should also decide *Where* to pray during the time you have set aside. Try to find places which are conducive to prayer.

Under *How*, list the techniques which will help you to be more successful in your praying. For example, if you've decided to pray while traveling in the car, but you find it hard to remember to do so, then write down that you will put a note on your dashboard. You might also write "Pray aloud" or "Pray silently with musical background to drown out distractions." *How* can also relate to the organization of your prayer. If you are an angry, serious person, you might write "Straightforward talk with God." If you are a methodical person, you might put down that you will keep a record of your prayer requests and God's answers.

You see, the whole point is to take some or all of those fifteen characteristics and see how they apply to your prayer life. If you are truly yourself when you pray, it ought to be much more enjoyable and natural. Then you should meet with greater success than you would if you were trying to follow some pattern which fits a personality considerably different from your own.

Section on Bible Study
Try to incorporate your personality into your study of the Scriptures. First read 2 Timothy 3:16-17, and meditate on God's purpose for putting his message down in written form so that we might read and study it. Then ask God to help you infuse your Bible study with your personality.

Under the sections *When* and *Where*, you can list those times and places that are conducive to study, taking into account your own unique personality.

Under the section *What*, you can list the content of your study. For example, since we have been studying how to be yourself with God, you might want to write that you will study those characteristics that you starred, trying to understand how they can be used righteously or unrighteously.

Under the section *How*, you can list the study methods you want to use, such as studying with a concordance and commentaries, taking notes, or any other kind of method that seems to fit with your personality and style.

Section on Obedience

After reading John 14:21 and meditating on it for a short while, then pray, asking that the Holy Spirit would make clear to you how your particular personality can be used in obeying God. In this exercise, you really need to pay attention to those fifteen starred characteristics. You are probably getting somewhat familiar with those characteristics by now.

The heading *What* can designate the focus for your obedience. It may be an area that God is asking you to develop to a greater degree of obedience. This focus changes periodically. You might also list what you want in the way of obedience. For example, I wrote down that I wanted more spontaneous submission to the assignments the Lord gives me, with far more willingness to "play it by ear."

For another example, I am a very practical person; thus, for me the *What* of obedience pertains to areas of Scripture I can really apply to my life. As the Holy Spirit makes something clear, practical, or sensible to me, then I try to focus on obeying that particular instruction from the Lord. The *What* section pertains to the areas the Lord wants you to improve in your obedience right now. When you respond to the *Attitude* section, again try to apply your fifteen personal characteristics. If you starred the characteristic of "active," then your attitude toward reaching a greater degree of obedience in that particular area might be one of enthusiasm.

In the *How* section, describe ways you can express your obedience to God in harmony with your personality. If you are "patient," your *How* might be to take a little longer time as you work toward a natural interaction with people you don't like very much.

Unfortunately, there is a tendency to feel we must pick one way as being the *right* way to be obedient (for example, in the area of accepting others). But with God, it's the bottom line that counts. God says to accept others, thereby bringing praise to him (Romans 15:7). With God, obedience expresses love. Remember the teaching of Matthew 21:28-31—a story of two sons who were requested to go into the field and work. One said to his father that he would go, but he didn't, while the other said he would not go, but then he changed his mind and went to work. The father was pleased only with the son who ended up doing what was requested.

Note to class leader:
Get some of the people in your class to share their answers with the rest of the class. Questions and struggles will naturally arise, which can mean personal growth for everyone.

My God-Given Characteristics

able to be alone	deliberate	jealous	polite
accepting	dependable	kind	pragmatic
active	dependent	knowledgeable	protective of
adaptable	determined	lenient	others
affectionate	devoted	liberated	prudent
afraid	dignified	likable	purposeful
angry	diligent	literary	quiet
anxious to please	diplomatic	lively	relaxed
appreciative	directive	logical	respected
articulate	even-tempered	loving	scientific
artistic	excited	loyal	self-controlled
attentive	exhilarated	masculine	serious
attractive	fair	mature	sincere
available	faithful	meditative	solicitous
brave	feminine	merciful	stable
calm	flexible	mild	stimulating
capable	friendly	modest	straightforward
careful	generous	motivated	strong
casual	gentle	obedient	submissive
cheerful	genuine	objective	supportive
comfortable	gracious	obliging	sympathetic
committed	grateful	observant	tenderhearted
compassionate	happy	optimistic	tolerant
concerned for	healthy	original	triumphant
people	helpful	patient	trusting
confident	honest	peaceable	understanding
conscientious	hopeful	perceptive	unrestrained
considerate	hospitable	persistent	used by others
consistent	humble	persuasive	vulnerable
contented	humorous	philosophical	willing
courageous	imaginative	pleasant	wise
courteous	impatient	pleased with	
creative	independent	others	
curious	intelligent	pleased with	
daring	involved	self	

Communication: The Key to a Personal Relationship With God

Prayer: I talk to God (Psalm 62:8).

When:

Where:

How:

Bible Study: God talks to me (2 Timothy 3:16-17).

When:

Where:

What:

How:

Obedience: I express my love for God (John 14:21).

What:

Attitude:

How:

8

STEP THREE:
STRONG ENOUGH TO SERVE

David said to Saul, "Let no one lose heart on account of this Philistine; your
servant will go and fight him."
Saul replied, "You are not able to go out against this Philistine and fight him;
you are only a boy, and he has been a fighting man from his youth."
But David said to Saul, "Your servant has been keeping his father's sheep.
When a lion or a bear came and carried off a sheep from the flock, I went
after it, struck it and rescued the sheep from its mouth. When it turned on me,
I seized it by its hair, struck it and killed it. Your servant has killed both the
lion and the bear; this uncircumcised Philistine will be like one of them,
because he has defied the armies of the living God."
1 Samuel 17:32-36

Life is a process of discovery. We are all explorers as we go
through the many challenges of life. Because we are all born with
certain unique, God-given strengths, because we are creatures of
God, we have a vast potential within. We have, in fact, been made
in the image of God himself.

But many people do not feel a sense of adventure in their lives.
They are not interested in discovering and developing their innate
strengths. Amazingly enough, even some people within the church
are not interested in exploring their own potential, in knowing exactly what natural capabilities their Creator has given them. They
seem to fear themselves, for the idea of self-discovery makes them
think that they are perhaps being self-centered. Because they do
not want to seem proud, they overreact by neglecting the skills and
talents God has given them to use. It is as if they prefer inactivity
and false humility to a uniquely challenging ministry of their own—
a life which should be a beautiful adventure for them because it was
custom-designed by God.

Each of us is able to do many things. However, in comparison to the things we cannot do, they are few. The world has become so complex, and the body of knowledge has grown so much, that we are limited as to what we can do well, perhaps more by lack of time than by lack of ability. Some people say that time is the scarcest commodity of all.

Scripture tells us to use our time wisely (Psalm 90:12, Ephesians 5:15-16, and Colossians 4:5). God helps us use our time efficiently by giving us certain personal strengths that stand out among the rest of our abilities. Those strengths, when used righteously, are significant, God-designed tools for us to use in his work.

Realizing Your Own Strength

Step three in the development of your godly self-respect is a step of self-realization. God has given you certain strengths you carry about with you. They are points you have in your favor. It is important to sit down and consider what your God-given strengths are. Then you will begin to see how you can put that godly potential into action.

We all need to appreciate our strengths and determine to use each of them for God's ministry to others. God created us for ministry. He is in the business of ministering to others through us. Since your strengths are God-given, they are naturally effective in service to the Lord.

God would not normally give us an assignment unless he had already provided the ability to perform it. How unfortunate it is when we do not even know what our abilities are. For then, as life rolls on before us, we do not even recognize the tasks for which we have been prepared. Since God is not in the business of sending telegrams, we must be able to recognize, along the path of our daily walk with him, those situations which match our strengths. They will be the telegrams that call us into action.

To know our strengths and to feel comfortable, even *good* about them, is critically important for an effective ministry. If God had given me a snowplow to use for my neighbors here in Colorado Springs, wouldn't I be irresponsible if I didn't even know it was in my driveway? Obviously I should recognize the gift of the snowplow and be ready to use it when it snows. In the same way I should feel good about the personal strengths God has given me, being prepared to use them whenever I am given the opportunity.

But unfortunately the church is full of people who believe it is sinful to feel good about yourself. But what is wrong with acknowledging a spiritual reality? What is wrong with recognizing your strengths, feeling good about them, and using them to serve God?

The argument of self-condemnation seems to stem from certain passages of Scripture which emphasize the importance of humility. For example:

> Do nothing out of selfish ambition or vain conceit, but in humility consider others better than yourselves. Each of you should look not only to your own interests, but also to the interests of others. (Philippians 2:3-4)

These verses do not teach that having positive feelings about yourself inevitably causes unrighteous pride. We need to recognize that there exists both an unrighteous pride and a righteous pride.

The negative reaction of certain Christians to all forms of self-respect probably comes out of the widespread negative reaction to twentieth century humanism. It is popular in this humanistic age to be exceedingly self-serving. Boastful pride is the way of this world. Many conscientious Christians, recognizing the unholiness of such self-striving, understandably disapprove of this humanistic pride.

But why is it necessary to always react negatively when people speak confidently of their abilities? There is no reason to go totally overboard. What we need is some real spiritual wisdom if we are to respond with true godliness. In order to get *God's* perspective, let's take a look at some biblical teaching which calls for righteous pride and confidence.

Your Self-Confidence in God

The kind of pride which is encouraged in Scripture is a *righteous* pride. When we have this kind of pride, we are free to evaluate ourselves objectively as we serve God. In the words of Paul, "Each one should test his own actions. Then he can take pride in himself, without comparing himself to somebody else, for each one should carry his own load" (Galatians 6:4-5). There is a righteous pride which comes from self-examination done in communication with God. Our pride should always be in the context of the Lord (Jeremiah 9:24, 1 Corinthians 1:31, and 2 Corinthians 10:17).

There is one critical rule to follow in order to prevent righteous pride from becoming unrighteous: *Do not arrive at good feelings about yourself by comparing yourself with or feeling superior to someone else.* Feelings of superiority are a sure sign of unrighteous pride.

The human mind is not capable of judging the superiority of actions. Only God can see the whole picture. All of the assignments he has given have value. In this sense, my task of writing this book is no more important than your task of reading it. Each of us is merely doing the task assigned by God with the equipment he has given us. There is really no basis for self-pride—only for the sober acknowledgment that all the good things we have *originate* in God's designing of tasks and *end* in his glory.

It is not unrighteous pride to admit you have a few significant strengths with which to serve God. It's okay to feel good about yourself for being chosen by God to contribute something to his work. The confidence this service gives you is considerably different than the feeling of proud superiority you get when you compare yourself with others. It is also different than commending yourself. In the long run, the only commendation that really counts is that which comes from the Lord. "For it is not the man who commends himself who is approved, but the man whom the Lord commends" (2 Corinthians 10:18).

Not only is boasting unrighteous, but it cancels out the Lord's commendation. Scripture clearly states that if we boast of our own actions in front of other people, that will be the only reward we get (Matthew 6:1-8). I know a great number of times when I have canceled out my heavenly reward by comparing myself with and determining myself to be better than someone else. And there were those times when I took all the credit for an accomplishment, foolishly forgetting that all that I am is from God, and that *he* is a partner in everything I do.

The Lord taught us that we should be humble. But how far does true humility go? Should we deny the good qualities God has placed within us? No! Instead we should consider true humility to be a recognition that the good things we have received are from God's hand. For a significant portion of our being is not of our own doing, and thus we should not take credit for it.

Consider this Scripture passage (if you are like me, you have overlooked applying it to yourself): "Finally, brothers, whatever is true, whatever is noble, whatever is right, whatever is pure, whatever is lovely, whatever is admirable—if anything is excellent or praiseworthy—think about such things" (Philippians 4:8). Many people consider the mountains, streams, wild animals, and so on, when they read this passage. And yet they do not consider *people*—including themselves—in this category. I'm not talking about the sins of mankind, but rather about the positive aspects which come from God.

If you will allow yourself to feel good about who you are and what you can do for God, and if you can implement this passage in your thinking about yourself for a period of six months, I am convinced that many Scriptures will jump out at you to challenge your lack of self-confidence and self-respect. You will soon see the proof in Scripture that you have been wrongly judging yourself. You will see that God is urging you to get in touch with all that he made you to be.

What the world needs now is confident Christians. Certainly the world needs more love. But God has already provided enough love for the needs of the whole world (John 3:16). Within his wisdom and his right to choose, God has determined that his love should now be expressed through his people.

Unfortunately, God's people have a large dose of inadequate self-confidence, and so the love stays bottled up under the guise of humility. Sometimes it seems as if the sin of excessive self-depreciation is even greater than the sin of pride. At other times I wonder if such self-depreciation isn't just pride disguised. The people of God need a self-confidence that will keep them from shirking their spiritual responsibilities—a self-confidence anchored in God himself.

It is spiritually important to feel confident. In fact Scripture shows us that there will be eternal results: "Do not throw away your confidence; it will be richly rewarded. You need to persevere so that when you have done the will of God, you will receive what he has promised" (Hebrews 10:35-36). Here we see that confidence is valuable because it is necessary for perseverance. It is no easy job to do God's work in a rebellious world. Christians too often seek the easy way out. We have become addicted to comfort and pleasure. We have ceased to be in continual battle for the Lord.

Therefore, our lack of self-confidence harms us greatly, for it keeps us from wanting to be in the action. We rarely consider that the gain of comfort for ourselves may be far outweighed by the loss of glory for the Lord. We should be proud to be serving and even suffering for our Lord. The confident apostle Peter tells us, "If you suffer as a Christian, do not be ashamed, but praise God that you bear that name" (1 Peter 4:16).

Confident Humility

You may be wondering how you can keep yourself in check so you won't become unrighteously proud. First, I would suggest you do a word study on *pride*, keeping in mind the material in this chapter. Second, remember that your competence comes from God (2 Corinthians 3:5), and that all that you are and do is from his power. He created you and gives you the energy to do good according to his will. In this way, when you are tempted to feel proud, self-righteous, or self-made, then you will remember with humility your God-made, God-powered design.

Whatever *is* superior about ourselves is due to God's power working in us. For example, it is not necessarily a great personal achievement for a person who has been raised in a Christian home not to swear. A new Christian who has been brought up in a home where profanity is frequently used may occasionally slip with an unintentional curse word. The Christian who does not swear should be careful not to feel self-righteous, for he has little about which to boast. His non-swearing is no struggle—the deck has been stacked in his favor. He needs to remember this in order to avoid comparing himself with someone else (which is forbidden in Galatians 6:4-5), so that he will not become unreasonably proud of his righteousness. Instead he should have a godly sense of confident humility.

We need to be more concerned about our own ministry for the Lord than we are about the ministry of someone else. We can learn a lot from an incident which happened shortly before the Lord Jesus ascended into heaven (John 21:15-23). There was Jesus, discussing Peter's future with him. All of a sudden, Peter turned and saw John following them. So Peter decided to ask the Lord what would happen in the future to his friend John. Jesus' simple answer was, "What is that to you? You must follow me." Clearly our eyes must be on Jesus and not on someone else. We should not compare either our strengths or our ministries with those of others.

Amazing as it seems, we can each keep our eyes on Jesus to follow him, even though we all walk different roads. We follow an omnipresent God who walks an infinite number of paths, but we are to focus our minds on his singular presence with each of us. His true disciples deny themselves and take up their crosses into all parts of the world.

Although Jesus' disciples should be concerned about the work of other disciples and should express this concern in prayer, financial support, and other forms of assistance, we should never take part in a judgmental comparison of ministries. Praise and thanks be to God that there is no room for competition in the body of Christ. Each one of us has a task (1 Corinthians 3:5), and each of us has competence to perform that significant task (2 Corinthians 3:5). Sure folly it would be to compete, using our competence for someone else's task.

Competence is not always what we might consider to be excellence. If a certain ministry is your designated task from God, you may not consider yourself to be the best at performing that task. But perhaps God didn't want it done to the highest degree of excellence as much as he wanted it done with your particular style. I've often seen someone with far less competence than someone else accomplish far more than that other person could have done.

God understands all the complex interactions of billions of people. As we move through our lives, he perfectly matches us with people and tasks. He has the grand view of things. And throughout the scope of that grand view, he uses us in teams. If our eyes are on Jesus and our hearts are focused on love for God—a bond of love which leads to obedience—we will each accomplish a significant part of the team effort.

We are supposed to storm together the gates of hell (Matthew 16:18), and so we need to have confidence in one another and in the gifts God has given to each of us. If you want to see God's power in the church, you should avoid competitiveness, and when you boast, you should boast about the Lord and about what your brothers and sisters in the Lord have done. Your pride must focus on the team and on each member—including yourself—who does his part. Each member of God's team needs to feel competent, confident, and valuable in order to operate at full effectiveness. We should always remember that our self-confidence looks outward as well as inward.

Make Your Strengths Stronger

How can we begin to use our personal strengths? What's the first move? Certainly we need to identify what motivates us, as well as the areas in which we motivate others. Furthermore, by brainstorming and keeping a good list of all the things we are able to do, we can easily conclude what we *enjoy* doing. The value of focusing on these abilities which are the strongest and most enjoyable is that we can then go on to perfect those abilities throughout our lives.

The Scripture tells us to "live up to what we have already attained" (Philippians 3:16). We should not only want to hold on to the progress we have made, but we should desire to continue learning how to use our abilities in order to be a sharp cutting edge in service to the living God. If you do something well, then continue to do it better and better. When we consider ministry, variety may not be the spice of life—consistency may be of higher eternal value.

For example, some people have the strength of being able to talk to strangers without anxiety and with great personal effectiveness. Does the church need this skill? Certainly! Why couldn't friendly people who are not already working in the church be assigned the function of greeting visitors? Such friendliness would inevitably spread—it would be contagious.

A church could significantly benefit if the twenty most friendly people were used to reach out to new or shy people in the church for a commitment of a full year. Although we should all have a spirit of hospitality (Romans 12:13, 1 Peter 4:9), we all have different degrees of strength in the area of friendliness. Those who are timid and shy can benefit greatly by having a friend who is outgoing. The shy person, on the other hand, may very well add a different dimension or strength to the friendly person's life.

Do you have the ability to fix cars? Perhaps you are able to do it and you greatly enjoy it. The front of your house resembles a used car lot. God gave you the knack, and so you fix cars in your spare time. Here is a God-given strength to be used for others.

If you work on only your own cars, perhaps you are selfishly hindering your own godly self-respect. Your personal completeness will come only as you serve others by fixing their cars, or serving them in whatever your areas of strength may be. Therefore, it is only right and proper for you to offer (even to advertise) your skill to some members of the body of Christ.

Find some people like myself who have no mechanical ability, but who are overextending themselves in some ministry of the church. Go to them and say, "I'm able to fix cars. God gave me that ability to share with other people. If you ever need my services, please let me know, and I'll fix your car for the cost of the parts." If you have the financial means, you might even offer to pay for the parts if the person is poor.

Maybe you're terrific at housecleaning and you really enjoy it. In fact, maybe you work as an accountant at a desk in an office all week, but you also like housecleaning. You find that it takes you away from the pressures of the office, and you can do it rather automatically, leaving your mind in a peaceful state. That may be a strength given to you for service to others. So in your free time you could clean someone else's house.

Or perhaps you're good at graphic arts, so you could offer to make posters and design advertisements for the church. As a result, perhaps more people would come to seminars at your church. Your participation in the body of Christ and its growth would be as significant in God's sight as the teaching at the seminars. After all, without the use of your gift, fewer people would come to the seminar, and thus fewer people would grow spiritually.

The important thing to remember is that God designed your abilities largely in light of what he wants you to do in the world. As I walk along the path of my life, certain situations arise which call for my unique abilities. In those situations, I can see God calling each of my strengths, at various times, into action.

When I see a car broken down on a well-traveled road, I never stop. Why? Because I know that God has not given me the ability of fixing cars! (If I stopped, the people having car problems would really be in trouble, and then, furthermore, someone with mechanical abilities might pass them by.)

But when I see someone distressed in life, someone with serious personal problems, I try to stop for as much time as I can make available. I really want to lend a hand, because God has given me the ability to counsel. In this way I recognize that I am God-designed for his work through me.

Some people have very unique strengths which can be used in very unique situations. For example, a person who plays professional football can visit children who are sick, or speak out for Christ in a special way.

Most of us possess certain strengths which match the essential needs of others—cooking, cleaning, sewing, fixing cars, encouraging people, etc. These abilities are, in fact, blessings from God. It is our responsibility to reckon how important it is for our lives and for our hurting world to put our own potential into action. For only then do our strengths really become stronger.

In step two we dealt with how God has created us with our own unique personalities so that we may walk with him, giving him variety in his fellowship with mankind. God enjoys not only different cultures, but also tremendous variety in personalities. He wants *us* to enjoy variety, too. And so he has empowered us with certain personality characteristics to serve other people. Each person has strengths which fit nicely together with the needs of others. This is a part of the harmony God intended for mankind.

At the end of step two, you chose fifteen words to describe basic personal qualities you could incorporate in your walk with God. As we now consider step three, consider those same qualities in the context of your strengths. Because people are created to be interdependent, some of them need *you*. Sometimes people become lonely because they have been neglected. But even loneliness is a gift of God when it points people to the reality of their need for other people.

Many people are living their lives outside of God's will by deliberately keeping themselves away from other people. Human beings were not meant to live this way. They were meant to be together and to minister to each other through their different personalities and abilities. Your character traits exist not only for your walk with God (step two), but also for your interactions with people in the church, as well as with those who do not know God personally.

Upon those who do not believe in him, God wishes to send, along with the sun and the rain (Matthew 5:45, Acts 14:17), other, more personal aspects of his goodness. In this way he can at least make their lives more satisfying through the character traits of his own people—you and me. Even though unbelievers have chosen against a relationship with God, he can still love them through us. Paul puts this matter in perspective when he says, "Thanks be to God, who always leads us in triumphal procession in Christ and through us spreads everywhere the fragrance of the knowledge of him. For we are to God the aroma of Christ among those who are being saved and those who are perishing" (2 Corinthians 2:14-15).

It is important to create righteous outlets for your personality characteristics. If you are like me, you must convert your anger into righteous anger. For when you use your strengths in a righteous way, then you vitalize the body of Christ in the battle to tear down and rip apart the strongholds of Satan.

Examples of Strengths in the Bible
It may be helpful for us to take a look at the strengths of some of the great heroes of the faith to see how they put their potential into action. They certainly were aware of the strengths given them by God for his work in the world, and they used them as they were given opportunity.

David faced Goliath with a sling and a righteous *anger* (1 Samuel 17:32-58). Early in his life he saw that God had given him great ability with the sling, and he practiced to perfect it. He used this skill routinely in his care of the sheep, and he kept it fine-tuned and ready for any use God might have for it.

When David heard Goliath mocking the Israelites, his righteous anger led him to a decision to silence Goliath's insults against the Lord God. David did not take stock of all the weapons available to him. He had a skill and he knew it was given to him by God precisely for this moment in history. He may not have been the strongest man in the Israeli camp, but this was the task for which God had well equipped him. His small size may actually have relaxed Goliath to the point that the giant's reflexes would not bring his shield to protect his head. And at the same time David's sling outmaneuvered and overcame the brute force of the giant's arm and sword. Truly David was prepared by God for that moment in history!

If you have a sense of righteous *determination*, like Joshua and Caleb you will be anxious to do God's assignment according to his timing (Numbers 13:30, 14:6-9). Thus you will be able to expediently carry out God's solution to a crippled church and to a hurting world.

Elijah's righteous *jealousy* led him to take on the prophets of the false god Baal. And his righteous anger can be observed in his bold confrontation with those prophets (1 Kings 18:16-40).

Jonah's *bravery* and *ability to talk to strangers* was, after an unrighteous detour, finally available for righteous use. As a result, many people in the city of Nineveh were saved (Jonah 3:3-10).

Abraham's *generosity* led him to give his nephew Lot the better choice of land (Genesis 13:5-13). Later Lot was saved from death when, by that same, great concern for others, Abraham convinced God to save some people before destroying Sodom, Gomorrah, and the entire plain (Genesis 18:16-19:29).

Concern for people was a very significant personality strength in Levi. Immediately after turning from tax corruption to follow Jesus Christ, he personally invited his sinner friends to dinner where the guest of honor was the one and only Messiah (Luke

5:27-32). Levi's loving concern for the salvation of others brought many sinners into contact with the Savior.

Dorcas's *compassion* for hurting people was greatly used by the Lord and cherished by the believers in the early church (Acts 9:36-41). Her personality strengths helped many people.

The apostle John's *tenderness* was used by God to write stirring words about the Lord's tender love for us. We can observe the compassionate spirit of John in his gospel account and especially in his letters at the end of the New Testament.

Example upon example could be given of God-given strengths used in his service. But we do not need to appeal to Scripture for our examples. You and I should be able to project ourselves into this list of examples. We too are disciples of the Lord.

What we learn from Ephesians 2:10 is powerfully correct: God *is* at work, turning each of us into creative instruments in his service. He wants us to work together in harmony upon the stage of human history, to bring down the walls of evil with the great proficiency of our combined lives. "When the trumpets sounded, the people shouted, and at the sound of the trumpet, when the people gave a loud shout, the wall collapsed; so every man charged straight in, and they took the city" (Joshua 6:20).

Let's shout for victory in the name of our Lord, the one God of the whole universe! For God prepares his people, men and women from all nations, to serve him in righteousness, power, and love through the strengths he places within each of us individually. He takes those strengths and wraps them together in a body called the church, which is then strong enough to march, with a renewed sense of self-respect, against the very gates of hell.

Questions for study and discussion

1. How does it feel to be powerfully equipped to serve God at his bidding?

2. Are you at the place where you can look forward with peaceful excitement (rather than anxiety) to difficult assignments from the Lord? Explain.

3. Do you think it is wrong to feel good about your strengths? Explain.

4. Romans 12:10 states, "Be devoted to one another in brotherly love. Honor one another above yourselves." Think of some Christian friends or members of your small group. Write down some of their names and some strengths you see in them. Then describe how you can honor each of these people.

5. What is your reaction to Galatians 6:4-5, especially the phrase, "Then he can take pride in himself . . ."? What is the difference between righteous and unrighteous pride?

6. Meditate on Philippians 4:8 as it applies to your view of yourself. After ten minutes of prayerful reflection, what is your response? In light of this verse, make a list of all the positive spiritual things you want to think about this week, and set aside a time each day to meditate on them.

7. What teaching in this chapter affected your thinking most of all? Explain.

Work sheet instructions for: "My God-Designed Strengths"

The Left Column ("My God-Designed Strengths")
Meditate on these Scriptures: 2 Corinthians 3:5 and 9:8, Galatians 6:4-5, Ephesians 2:10 and 4:7, Philippians 1:6, and Hebrews 10:35-36. Then begin writing your strengths or abilities in the left-hand column as quickly as they come to your mind. You should eventually be able to list items all the way down this page and have to go on to a supplementary sheet.

Some participants might find it difficult to get started because they are used to having such a low opinion of themselves. If this is your situation, do not despair. The fact that you do not know what your abilities are does not mean that you do not have very many of them. In fact, God is so creative and loving toward you and so eager for you to be involved in his work in the world and in the church, that he has gifted you with *many* abilities. You may be blinded with fear that you would become proud, but if this is the case, pride is the last thing to which you will be vulnerable.

Just prayerfully ask for the Lord's help to know your abilities without becoming puffed up. Remember 1 Corinthians 8:1, which says, "Knowledge puffs up, but love builds up." Knowledge alone of your abilities will puff you up; but it is the intention of this work sheet to help you know your strengths *in order to use them for others*. As you take this knowledge and put it into action, using your competence to meet the needs of others, you will be loving others. And as you love them, you will build them up and also build *yourself* up in the Lord. Be open and honest—try not to censor your responses.

If you have extreme difficulty filling in this column of your abilities, then you need to give it to your family or your friends and have them fill it out. They know what you are good at, and they know where they would use your strengths. Explain to them what you are doing—that you are working on developing a godly self-respect and that you need to get in touch with those areas in which you have unique talent. Tell them that it's not a very comfortable thing for you to list your personal assets. You might want to ask them to think about it for a week, and then you can get back with them. That way, they will have thought it through very carefully, and whatever they tell you should have some real validity.

You have probably wondered how to use the little boxes to the left of the strengths you have listed. You should put a *check mark* inside the box of any of those strengths you have clearly communicated to others so that they might feel free to call upon you in these areas of your ministry. Of course, you will continually need to be communicating these abilities to others, so that they know that you are willing to put them into service. People do not automatically know what you are willing to do, even though you may be using those abilities openly. Often they do not see your efforts. Since they can't observe you, they have no way of knowing that you are offering yourself to them in the areas of your abilities.

Put a *star* in a box after you have gone to the church leadership and stated that God seems to have gifted you with this ability which you would like to use for the benefit of the church. Do not star it if you have only hinted at it; only star it if you have stated it very clearly to one or more members of your church leadership (for example, members of the church board, elders, deacons, pastor, etc.).

Those boxes which remain unmarked are the areas where you still need to let people know that God has given you some strengths you are willing to share. Determine to do this when you feel God is calling you to be of help.

The Right Column ("People Who May Need My Ministry of These Strengths")

Next to each ability, write the names in the right-hand column of people who could use your services in that particular area. For example, let's suppose that one of your skills is an excellent mechanical ability with washing machines. Then in this right-hand column you would write the names of those people you know who have two left hands when it comes to mechanical ability, especially if they have limited financial resources. Now if you don't know anyone who needs this assistance, then you might put down "Tell the deacons of my ability." Then speak to the deacons about your willingness and your skill.

If, on the other hand, one of your abilities is talking to rebellious teenagers, then think of your acquaintances and people in your church, and write down the names of those who have teenagers who are somewhat rebellious or on the fringe. If you do not know who those families are, you might ask your pastor or some of your close friends in the church. The important thing is to know that you have something God has given to you and then to determine to use your ability to glorify God.

God expects you to use your strengths when they are needed. You can derive a great deal of satisfaction and godly self-respect if you work to use yourself as a God-designed person in certain kinds of ministries. So fill this right-hand column out as completely as you can, and then continue to fill it out over the next fifty years, as the Lord brings people to your mind or as you get more information from your church leadership.

My God-Designed Strengths

	My God-Designed Strengths	People Who May Need My Ministry of These Strengths
☐		
☐		
☐		
☐		
☐		
☐		
☐		
☐		
☐		
☐		

9

STEP FOUR:
THE ADVANTAGE OF
WEAKNESSES

He said to me, "My grace is sufficient for you, for my power is made perfect in weakness." Therefore I will boast all the more gladly about my weaknesses, so that Christ's power may rest on me.

2 Corinthians 12:9

A unique factor in Christianity is its emphasis upon *weakness*. We learn in our theology that God humbled himself to become one of his own creatures, that man gains his salvation only through the submissive acknowledgment that he is incapable of saving himself, that spiritual greatness comes only through humble servanthood, and so on.

But the weakness emphasized in Christianity should not be confused with the quality of feebleness, ineptitude, and disgrace we often associate with the word "weakness." It is, for example, not a spiritual liability but rather an asset to be truly humble. Furthermore, because human beings are merely creatures with built-in limitations, we inevitably have certain personal areas which are not totally perfect. In this sense, Christians ought to be very realistic—we should know our own limitations *and* the advantages which they offer us.

Granted, sin is a spiritual disease—a weakness that serves as a plague upon all of us. And yet this sickness is in the process of being healed within the kingdom of God by the King himself. Jesus

Christ is able and ready to heal the church of its sickness. Moreover, he wants us to take those personal weaknesses which have nothing to do with sin and use them to our advantage, instead of feeling inferior and ineffective because of them. Using our weaknesses to our advantage means using them to the advantage of his body, the church.

In the preceding chapter, we considered personal strengths. We often have the tendency to consider our strengths as a great blessing, but our personal weaknesses as a curse—a handicap of the soul. But that's not the biblical view. Let's take a close look at what God has to say about our weaknesses. After we take this fourth step in our progression, we should have a more optimistic perspective of ourselves and a new, unique dimension in our self-respect.

When we consider our weaknesses from a biblical viewpoint, we are confronted with the fascinating world of the kingdom of God. God gives us strengths largely for the direct benefit of others, but he gives us our weaknesses for our own great advantage. If we were to do it our way, we would possess no weaknesses—only strengths. And we certainly wouldn't consider our weaknesses as exceedingly beneficial. But God does things *his* way, and weaknesses are very special gifts from him. As we find contentment in the way God designed us—including our weaknesses—we can grow spiritually. For "godliness with contentment is great gain" (1 Timothy 6:6).

In this chapter, we shall be dealing with three beneficial purposes of our weaknesses or inabilities: (1) our weaknesses can keep us away from the wrong ministries and thereby save us time and energy; (2) our weaknesses allow God's power to work through us so that we might have daily evidence of his presence with us; and (3) our weaknesses can keep us interdependent with others within the church, giving us more complete lives. But before we embark upon these three areas, let's first take a look at depression—a weakness on top of a weakness.

Escaping Depression: Setting the Prisoner Free

Far too many people in the church are suffering from *depression*. Although there are many different causes of depression, one major cause is a negative attitude about oneself. Instead of analyzing negative feelings and making plans to do something about a problem, a person who is depressed holds his negative feelings inside, avoiding exposure of his problems to others. The result is that many people feel worthless without even thoroughly knowing *why*.

Depression can go back to an unhappy childhood, an unrewarding marriage, or some other negative situation in a person's life. Unfortunately, depression can spread like an emotional cancer through lack of energy and feelings of worthlessness. It is a weakness which multiplies—a weakness on top of another weakness. For, in the case of depression, a simple personality weakness or negative experience can become unnecessarily compounded.

Instead of growing stronger through suffering as the Bible advises, depressed people grow weaker. People who experience depression feel so poorly about themselves that they often do not expect to be able to do anything within the ministry of the church. This negative plague of depression can be battled only through a positive approach to ourselves.

In step one, we considered the special care God has taken in our creation—the fact that God doesn't make junk. He created us just the way he wanted us to be, and in doing so he had in mind certain special assignments for each of us. In step two, we considered the fact that each of us can walk with God in a genuine way. In other words, each of us can pray, study the Bible, and obey God straight from our own personalities, rather than attempting to act like someone else. Then, in step three, we observed the importance of the strengths God gave us for ministry to other people.

So up to this point we have been focusing on areas which are more positive, in which we can all have some good feelings. Even a depressed person can focus on what we have studied so far and make some progress against his depression. The more a person can begin to use his positive areas for the benefit of others, the more his depression might subside.

However, there are some people who can do lots of good things for others and yet continue to put themselves down, either by minimizing their own strengths or by focusing on their inabilities and sins. This chapter and the following two chapters can help depressed people find a new way of dealing with both inabilities and sins.

Many people experience worthlessness because they think they ought to be able to do *all things*. They have never seriously considered the fact that God does not expect them to be able to do everything. Then there are others who refuse to accept themselves until they are perfectly *sinless*. In so doing, they set standards for themselves which no one but Christ himself has ever achieved. Even God loved and accepted us while we were yet sinners (Luke 5:32, 15:1-2, John 3:16, and Romans 5:8); thus we need to do that with ourselves as well.

Depression is one of Satan's best tools to keep the church weak, operating at less than peak effectiveness. I would urge you not to let Satan get away with it. Determine to do something about that depression—to act *positively* for the Lord, because in his eyes you are very special.

If your depression persists, then there may be other factors in your life which are keeping you from dealing with some negative feelings. In this case, it would be wise for you to seek out the help of a Christian counselor. If your depression is longstanding and severe, I would suggest that you seek out the services of a Christian psychotherapist or a professional Christian counselor with at least a few years of experience.

Avoiding the Detours

Let us deal now with the first of the three ways in which our weaknesses help us: *our inabilities keep us from choosing the wrong ministries.* If you agree with me that the greatest happiness is serving God in the place where he wants us to serve, doing his great pleasure in our lives, then you will immediately recognize the benefit of weaknesses. For the fact is, there are otherwise too many things to do in life.

If there were no limitations on our abilities, it would then be impossible to decide how to spend our time—whether for ourselves or for others. Life would be truly confusing. So many choices of what to do with our time would paralyze us into inaction. Our weaknesses prevent us, in a very natural way, from being thus over-whelmed with the frustration of what to do. The fact that our strengths are far outnumbered by our weaknesses narrows our options of what we should do with our lives to a more reasonable scope.

Whereas our strengths point us to the right ministries, our weaknesses point us away from the wrong ministries. While God works through our weaknesses, he assigns our primary ministries based on our strengths. It is a built-in system of checks and balances.

Within a society that overemphasizes self-reliance, we can experience tremendous freedom in weakness. There appears to be an ingrained cultural message that we need to do all things well. This puts tremendous pressure on us, because it's impossible to do all things well without unreasonable effort.

The freedom to *not* do things in a society as busy as ours is a very welcome advantage to most people. With a limited amount of time and a seemingly unlimited number of responsibilities, we must choose daily to do a few things well, most things with average skill, and occasionally a few things poorly. Knowledge of our weaknesses can keep us from trying to do too much.

As a father, I know it is impossible for me to do all the things for my children that would be good to do. I have limitations of time, and, more importantly, I have limitations of ability. I see, on one hand, that God didn't intend me to do certain things with my children. And, on the other hand, I see that he has indeed given me certain abilities and opportunities to do some of the most important things with them. This is a tremendously liberating limitation. Although I cannot plan to do all things with my children, I do trust their complete development to the Lord's provision.

All cultures pass on their values through the socialization of children from the time of the early years. It is during that time that unrealistic, perfectionistic values—values not found in Scripture— are passed on to us. Through criticism, many of us learned in childhood that it is dangerous to make mistakes and dangerous to try new things. The lesson of perfectionism is that everything must be done with our very best effort, and even our best effort rarely produces a totally acceptable result. Thus, we come to believe there must be something wrong with us.

Some people determine in childhood that they are second-class citizens, born to serve their parents at their every whim. And so they conclude that they are duty-bound to others in general. Later, in adult life, they come to take responsibility for people even when those people don't want them involved in their lives, even when those people want to solve their own problems. If I were to burden myself by taking care of other people's problems, and, in doing so, cause them to become dependent on me, I would be robbing them of their own self-confidence.

Another incorrect message we tend to learn in childhood is that our personal worth depends on everybody liking us at all times. Because of this very common childhood obsession, many people can't handle conflict of any sort later on. They become exceedingly hypocritical, changing their opinions and actions constantly in order to avoid conflict and comply with the desires of others. This kind of avoidance of reality keeps people from walking with Jesus Christ, who taught us that in this life we will inevitably meet persecution.

People become trapped by these kinds of incorrect, unbiblical values and teachings from their culture. The mere inability to do things perfectly or in line with sinful, perfectionistic expectations robs them of self-respect. They don't feel free to accept their God-designed limitations. If you have some of these messages rolling around in your head—messages which are purely irrational but feel so terribly real—then it would be a good idea to list them. Then try to check them against reality.

Our perfect God understands us and often expects much less from us than we, who are imperfect, expect from ourselves. Although he desires us to move toward the ideal of perfection, he does not expect us to reach absolute perfection overnight (Matthew 5:48, Philippians 3:12-14, James 3:2, and 1 John 1:8-10). It's nice to have a God who understands that we are trapped in sin. He realized we were incapable of perfection in our fallen state, and so he gave us a way out of the penalty of our sin—a way that did not depend upon our own effort. He accepted us then at the cross, and he continues to accept us even now in our imperfection.

> You see, at just the right time, when we were still powerless,
> Christ died for the ungodly. Very rarely will anyone die for a
> righteous man, though for a good man someone might possibly
> dare to die. But God demonstrates his own love for us in this:
> While we were still sinners, Christ died for us. (Romans 5:6-8)

Since so much of our lack of self-acceptance comes from the conditional love of our parents, why not accept your parents as they are, or were, and realize the imperfection of their past messages to you? They, like you and I, were contaminated by sin when they raised us. Sin-contaminated people sometimes say things which hurt other people. It's an unfortunate fact of life. Consequently we need to stop living our lives based on ungodly, incorrect, perfectionistic messages from our past. Let's gather ourselves together emotionally and mentally in the present by taking on the merciful, healing perspective the Lord has of us, his body.

God knows that our efforts alone produce nothing but a kind of righteousness which resembles filthy rags (Isaiah 64:6). Thus he is all the more accepting of our frailty. Although our parents may have expected us to be strong in all circumstances and to show no signs of weakness (fear, disappointment, etc.), God knows our limitations. He wants us to call for his help, which means that we need to be in touch with our weaknesses, especially our emotional weaknesses.

In order to counter the negative effects still plaguing us from our past, it is important to take on a new, positive, objective way of living. The apostle Paul appeals to us with precisely this kind of spiritually revolutionary message.

> I urge you, brothers, in view of God's mercy, to offer your bodies as living sacrifices, holy and pleasing to God—which is your spiritual worship. Do not conform any longer to the pattern of this world, but be transformed by the renewing of your mind. Then you will be able to test and approve what God's will is—his good, pleasing and perfect will. (Romans 12:1-2)

In light of this Scripture, we should first offer our very lives—our bodies in living service—to be wholly God's, as a sign of our acknowledgment of his worthiness, greatness, majesty, and dominion over the earth and all that is in it. Secondly, we should offer our minds to God, allowing him to transform our thoughts to his thoughts. We need to keep a running dialogue with ourselves. When our subconscious self brings incorrect personal thoughts to mind, we begin to feel negative about ourselves. But we have to catch that uncomfortable feeling as soon as possible and begin to question the thought that causes us to feel so pessimistic. Only then can God rescue us by his truth, which we begin to store at that point in our memory.

Only when we yield ourselves to God will he give us the power to ignore our persistently negative thoughts and lead us into actions which are based on the truth. When we begin to act on God's truth rather than on the confining, ungodly messages that lurk in our memory, then we will experience a freedom and joy of deliverance from our own inner prison. We should thank God that he is more understanding of us than we are of ourselves.

This transformation process is not easy. But little by little victory can be gained. The renewing of one's mind at times comes spontaneously, and at other times only with a great deal of effort. But the battle is worth it. We need to go on—until we die—to purge from our minds those worldly thoughts that cause our lives to conform to the pattern of this fallen earth. The key to this perseverance is the desire to live for God, to worship him through a godly life.

It's time for us to stop holding back our godly self-respect, to stop discrediting ourselves. We cannot do everything perfectly. We cannot meet standards imposed on us by our families and our culture. God is the only one who understands us well enough to lay *realistic* expectations on us, and he is the only one who has the right to do so, because he bought us with a price (1 Corinthians 6:19-20, 7:23).

Maybe you've been putting yourself down for a long time because you can't do things God really didn't require of you in the first place. God probably doesn't expect you to make pies like Aunt Martha, or to have a spotless home like your mother, or to get the top grades in your college class. Maybe God didn't want you to be beautiful, because he had a ministry for you which would require someone who would not intimidate others with physical beauty. Maybe God made you clumsy so that you'd be more human, more able to capture the hearts of the common person. And the list of examples could go on and on.

I remember when my daughter Becky was four years old, racing with some children in the neighborhood, and she came in last place. I remember my heart sinking to see that my daughter wouldn't be as athletic as I was. And then God broke into my disappointment within the minute, saying to me, "My dear, earthly father of Becky, do you remember yesterday when a two-year-old fell and hurt himself and our Becky was the first one there?" And thus I was exposed to my foolishness. For I was quite sure that I would rather have a daughter quick to compassion than quick in athletics.

Some parents, with their unrealistic expectations for their children, try to take over the control of their children's lives. They forget that their children belong to *God*, and that he and he alone has the right and the power to determine the course of their lives.

Many people who put down others also put down themselves. Perhaps you have been belittling yourself for some weakness you were born with. That's an unrealistic expectation—something you need to deal with. Why don't you just stop and search your mind, laying open to the exposure of the Holy Spirit all the negative feelings about yourself which have nothing to do with sin. The difference between a weakness and a sin is that a sin is an act of violation against one of God's commands. But personal weaknesses are not prohibited in Scripture. I hope you will struggle to make this distinction clear in your thinking.

It is very difficult to live a godly life at the same time that you are cooperating with Satan's condemnations and accusations. Keep in mind from the book of Job that it is Satan's tendency to unjustly accuse us. Nothing could be more delightful to him than to see us cooperating with him. It is his aim to have men follow him rather than God. In falsely accusing ourselves, we follow Satan. That thought doesn't feel too comfortable, does it?

If you are struggling with this area of self-condemnation, try to clearly discern the source of your bad feelings about yourself. The source of your unrighteous self-condemnation could be your non-acceptance of your weaknesses—areas which God never intended to be strengths in your life. Take your eyes off the strengths of others, except as examples for you to follow or as sources of help. Make this a prayer to God, so that you will not feel bad when you see the strengths in others which God did not give to you. Do not be like the clay which talks back to the potter because it is dissatisfied with the way it was formed (Romans 9:19-21).

An Anchor for the Soul

A second great advantage of our weaknesses is that *they allow us to experience God's power in our lives on a daily basis.* Every day we are asked to do things for which we are not equipped. And every day some of those tasks come out much better than we know we can expect from our own efforts alone. Why? Because "The Spirit helps us in our weakness" (Romans 8:26, 38-39).

Of course, we can see this power of God at work only if we have accepted our weaknesses, only if we are not afraid to take a good look at them. If we insist on being strong and capable in all areas, we miss the powerful evidence of God walking alongside us. For we then tend to take credit for that which only he can really do in our lives. We need to remember that our weakness allows for his strength.

Whenever we yield to God's strength, we become stronger ourselves. But many times we tend to yield to his strength only when we are not relying on our own. Thus our weaknesses are actually advantages because they draw us to God. We cannot be independent of God and still expect to grow spiritually. Paul came to see this in his own life in a very profound way.

> To keep me from becoming conceited because of these surpassingly great revelations, there was given me a thorn in my flesh, a messenger of Satan, to torment me. Three times I pleaded with the Lord to take it away from me. But he said to me, "My grace is sufficient for you, for my power is made perfect in weakness." Therefore I will boast all the more gladly about my weaknesses, so that Christ's power may rest on me. That is why, for Christ's sake, I delight in weaknesses, in insults, in hardships, in persecutions, in difficulties. For when I am weak, then I am strong.
> (2 Corinthians 12:7-10)

Paul was a person with many strengths, but his weaknesses also came to play a major part in his spiritual growth. They gave him opportunities to grow closer to the Lord.

When you attempt to do something in an area of weakness, you are much more apt to ask God for help, and thus much more able to see his involvement in your success. If you had all strengths and no weaknesses, your tendency would be to rely on yourself rather than on God. In this sense your weaknesses act as an anchor for your soul. They keep you close to God.

It would be good for each of us to perform at least one significant task every day in which we knew that failure would come if God did not intervene. Then we would find daily evidence that God answers prayer. Even when we forgot to pray, we would still see that God's love is not quick to condemn, for he likes to walk beside his children and help us in our weakness. A personal sense of security would gradually blossom in all of us if we would simply develop such a lifestyle of regular reliance on God.

Many years ago I designed a residential treatment program for seriously disturbed adolescents and their families. It was a program designed to keep the young people from going to the state hospital. A six-month government grant was awarded, and I had no more than two months to hire a staff of thirty, train them, purchase a facility, and begin to show success before the next grant application would be due. Efforts to find a suitable building were frustrating, and soon almost impossible.

When I finally found a suitable building, with the excellent help of a realtor friend, I could not locate the one-and-only official authorized to give us a Colorado license. She lived in a little rural town, the location of which I did not know. She didn't answer my phone calls, and I couldn't reach her through official sources. I tried everything I could think of without success, until the last possible day when our board of directors was meeting to decide whether to purchase the building.

That morning at 7:00 a.m., I suddenly remembered God's part in this project. For two whole weeks I had forgotten to bring this prayer request to him. On the spot, I acknowledged my sinfulness and handed over the problem to him, because I had no power at this point to solve it. I was finally accepting my weakness and inability and God's strength and capability in this difficult situation.

Later that day, I went to consult at a home for delinquent boys. I was greeted by the administrator, who asked, "Guess who's just been here for a surprise inspection?" You guessed it! It was the woman I was trying to locate, and she was right across the road inspecting another boy's home in that rural community. Well, we had dinner together, she looked at the building and approved it, and thus we were able to go ahead full speed with our treatment program.

I asked the inspector why she had come to the Colorado Springs area that day. She replied that when she woke up at 7:00 a.m. that morning, she just had an urge to come to Colorado Springs, but she wasn't sure why. I told her why. And I was very thankful to God that day for my weaknesses. For I had clear evidence that our weaknesses draw us closer to him and that, in doing so, they make us stronger. "For when I am weak, then I am strong."

A Bonding Force Within the Body

I am truly interested in living the kind of life God wants for me as an individual. But I also want to live the way he wants in the area of the corporate life of the church. This is the third area of the advantages of our weaknesses. God deliberately created mankind to be incomplete. When God looked down on Adam in the Garden of Eden, he saw that Adam was as he had intended him to be—incomplete (Genesis 2:18-25). And so God created marriage so that man and woman might minister to each other and complement each other through their differences for the rest of their lives. He intended families to have that same basic kind of built-in interdependence.

In much the same way, God wants his people to live in interdependence with one another and dependence on him. Nowhere does Scripture state that we should live totally independent of other people or of God. Although self-sufficiency of the individual within the church is pursued diligently by many Christians, it is quite unbiblical and destructive to the body of Christ. Furthermore, ministry should not be thought of as something believers do autonomously, as a series of many detached, solo efforts. Only a church which *collectively* supports its individual members has the strength to march against any bastion of hell.

Therefore, my weaknesses are great gifts to me because they keep me perpetually incomplete—unable to live alone. I need other people and they need me. And people who are hurting need all of us, working together in harmony. "Each one should use whatever gift he has received to serve others, faithfully administering God's grace in its various forms" (1 Peter 4:10). You should commit yourself to people instead of things, going out with the team known as the church where each person has a function—as in a well-tuned orchestra—to do God's work in this world.

Only by recognizing our *need* for others—since we are not able to do everything by ourselves—will we be continually reminded that *God wants us to live interdependently with our brothers and sisters in Christ.* The society we live in does not encourage the consideration of this very great truth. But God does. And Paul, the apostle who saw the strength in weakness, describes to us this need within the body of Christ for mutual dependence.

> Now to each one the manifestation of the Spirit is given for the common good. . . . The body is a unit, though it is made up of many parts; and though all its parts are many, they form one body. . . . God has arranged the parts in the body, every one of them, just as he wanted them to be. . . . The eye cannot say to the hand, "I don't need you!" And the head cannot say to the feet, "I don't need you!" On the contrary, those parts of the body that seem to be weaker are indispensable, and the parts that we think are less honorable we treat with special honor. (1 Corinthians 12:7, 12, 18, 21-23)

May you get so caught up in the joy of a team effort for God that your focus will be more outward than inward. In the fellowship of many believers, you will obtain more help than you can get from yourself alone, and you will experience and receive more love and success than you can achieve by yourself—all within the grace and design of God himself. For weaknesses within the body act as a bonding force to hold it together.

We need to always keep in focus Paul's words: "Those parts of the body that seem to be weaker are indispensable." God has given our weaknesses for various reasons. People of the world consider their weaknesses to be liabilities. But the people of the Lord have a different perspective—we have confidence that our weaknesses are all areas to be used to our advantage. Thus we gain a new kind of godly self-identity which keeps us in harmony with God, his work, and his people.

Work sheet instructions for: "My God-Designed Weaknesses and Inabilities"

The Left Column ("My God-Designed Weaknesses")
1. Take a look at the work sheet at the end of this chapter. After you have prayed for God's guidance and help to list your weaknesses and inabilities without going into self-condemnation, and after you have meditated on the verses listed on the work sheet, then fill in the left-hand column by listing various things which you are unable to do. All of us could fill out list after list of weaknesses and inabilities. Try to focus on those inabilities which at various times in your life you have felt you should be able to do in order to be a valuable person.

   Unfortunately, many people feel they must be able to do certain things in order to be worthwhile. Many of these things could be rather ridiculous, but do not hesitate to put them down if they are very real to you. This is an opportunity for you to list those areas that may have held you back in your self-respect for many years. Try to think back through your life. Focus on those weaknesses that still continue to bother you. As you make your list, remember that God has designed many of these inabilities.

An inability, as I define it, is not sin. Everyone is unable to do certain things—things about which the Bible makes no command. This is what I mean by inabilities. If you are unable to be patient with an older person in your church after the service when he is trying to have a discussion with you, that is not an inability, but a sin. Although God may not be preparing you for a ministry to older people, he does expect you to be patient enough to show everyday Christian love.

Maybe you feel as if you need to know everything. If this is the case, list specific things you feel you should know. Perhaps you are going against your own grain by requiring yourself to know what to do in all situations. Maybe you want to know all of the time what other people expect of you, but you find that you just can't do it. Welcome to the human race! That's where all the rest of us are, too.

No one knows *everything* but God. So if you are plagued by a negative self-image just because you're not perfect, stop putting yourself down. As you list your God-designed inabilities, thank God for each of them. Even Adam in his perfection in the Garden of Eden could not know and do all things. In fact it was Adam and Eve's unwillingness to accept weaknesses—their lack of acceptance before and thankfulness to God that they were not designed to know and do all things—that caused them to sin. If they would have thankfully accepted their God-designed inabilities, they would have had no attraction to the forbidden tree.

Most people don't have as much trouble filling out this column as they do the column which asks for their strengths. But if you are having a little more trouble with this particular column, that could be a good sign. It might be an indication that you have accepted yourself as someone who is capable and competent. But you might still want to ask some of your closest friends or some of your family members what things they see you striving for which seem to be beyond your capability. Perhaps as they help you fill out this sheet, they too will begin accepting the fact that God has designed some weaknesses in all of us.

2. After you have completed the left-hand column, take note of the little boxes along the left side. Put a *check mark* in each of those boxes when you can truthfully say to God, "Thank you for giving me this weakness." Approach this assignment in an attitude of prayerful meditation. Then ask the Lord to help you accept each of these inabilities, so that soon you will be able to thank him for all of them.

The Right Column ("People Who Can Minister to Me in These Weak Areas")

Remember that God designed the church as an interdependent body of people. Even when they were perfect and had not yet sinned, Adam and Eve still needed each other, and they still had inabilities and limitations. They were created in this way so that the human race would be interdependent. Likewise, the church is to be made up of people who depend on one another and who work together to build each other up.

In your church there are people who can help you when you have a need in your areas of inability. For example, you might write in the left-hand column, as I would, "No ability in automobile mechanics." Then you should list in the right-hand column the names of a few people you know who have that mechanical skill. Perhaps they could minister to you if your car needs service. Do not be concerned at this point whether they would or not—you don't know until you ask them. They may not be willing to help you until they understand that God designed them with certain abilities to use for others. Make sure you let these other people know that you are not looking for a free handout. The last thing you want to do is take advantage of them. But let them know that you need them.

You will probably find that if you begin to search for people with certain talents, you will find them. If you are able to utilize their strengths, you will be of immeasurable value in helping them develop their own godly self-respect. Be sure that you are willing and available to help these people by offering to use your own strengths in their areas of weakness.

My God-Designed Weaknesses and Inabilities

Relevant Scriptures: Romans 2:11, 8:26, 9:20-21, 12:3, 2 Corinthians 12:7-10, Philippians 3:16, and 1 Timothy 6:6

	My God-Designed Weaknesses	People Who Can Minister to Me in These Weak Areas
☐		
☐		
☐		
☐		
☐		
☐		
☐		
☐		
☐		
☐		

10

STEP FIVE:
REFINED IN THE FIRE OF LIFE

We rejoice in the hope of the glory of God. Not only so, but we also rejoice in our sufferings, because we know that suffering produces perseverance; perseverance, character; and character, hope.

Romans 5:2-4

A person who follows Jesus Christ is like an athlete. He must go through a training process which is both painful and rewarding. The word *sanctification* is used to describe the spiritual growth process each Christian is called to go through—a spiritual journey which submits the strengths and weaknesses of each individual to the complex trials of life itself. Each spiritual journey is different because each person is different.

But perhaps we should picture our spiritual athlete not so much as a solitary long-distance runner, but as a team player. Each Christian must go through a unique training process in which he is directly, individually responsible to God. But, since it is difficult for anyone to live apart from the world of other people, we need to do our training alongside our brothers and sisters.

Step five in the development of self-respect focuses on *perseverance* during the process of spiritual growth. Even after you recognize your God-given design (step one), begin to walk in a disciplined way with God (step two), and accept your God-designed strengths (step three) and weaknesses (step four), you need daily, spiritual determination in order to pass each new test of faith, thus growing into maturity (James 1:2-4). Our self-confidence is anchored in God himself, who promises to support and empower us throughout our spiritual growth process.

Remember the Source of the Power

As we mature, through the guidance of the Holy Spirit, into the image of Christ (2 Corinthians 3:18), we gain a new kind of strength. We are being refined through the fire of life. But we must remember that we can feel really good about our spiritual accomplishments only because they are *team* accomplishments achieved together with God. We must never lose sight of the fact that God has accomplished his purposes through us, having excellently equipped us for his work. "May the God of peace . . . equip you with everything good for doing his will, and may he work in us what is pleasing to him, through Jesus Christ . . ." (Hebrews 13:20-21).

And so we seek to strike a balance: we want to give credit to God for all the good things we do, yet, at the same time, we cannot deny the goodness he has placed *in us*. The key is recognizing fully that all we are comes from the hand of God (with the exception of sin and evil). When we depreciate ourselves and feel worthless, we are often insulting the Creator, who states plainly in Scripture that he is working in us to equip us to do every good work he has planned for our lives: "Being confident of this, that he who began a good work in you will carry it on to completion until the day of Christ Jesus" (Philippians 1:6). Notice that there is a goodness developing inside us as God carries out his plan for our lives. Moreover, we can also have confidence that the goodness will grow and become more powerful throughout our entire lives.

The main point is that we must recognize that God is equipping us *thoroughly*. "God is able to make all grace abound to you, so that in all things at all times, having all that you need, you will abound in every good work" (2 Corinthians 9:8). Although the primary message in this passage is Paul's exhortation to give finances generously to the poor, it is clear that he is talking about something more. God wants his children to be tremendously successful in any good work to which he calls us. (Notice all of the superlatives in this passage.) He gives us the grace necessary to reach out to others in unconditional love. It doesn't matter how disgusting other people may be; we will be able to have compassion on them because we have first received such compassion from the hand of God.

We should not obsessively concern ourselves with our own needs as we move out to do God's work in the world. The promise in 2 Corinthians 9:8 is that he will give us all that we need for all things and at all times. But we must never forget that this provision of all grace is given so that we may successfully complete his assignments for our lives.

It should give you tremendous satisfaction to know that you are so special to God that he has included you as a servant *and a partner* in his work in the world. Furthermore, not only are you chosen for God's work in the world, but you are also fully equipped to be successful for that work and allowed to be an eyewitness of his power on a daily basis.

Accomplished athletes do not glory in an easy victory over a less competent opponent. Athletes strive to take on increasingly more competent teams. Why is it then that we who are on the Lord's team do not arduously seek out the more difficult victories over sin in the world?

Many passages in Scripture liken the Christian life to an athletic event, a race. As spiritual athletes we should seek out the difficult tasks. For then we would discover, through our intensified experience, that the Christian life is exciting and challenging.

But many of us lack confidence. We are fearful that we will be defeated. Have we not yet realized that the kingdom of God is radically different from the kingdom of the world? For Christians there is a joy and maturity that comes through suffering, whereas for unbelievers suffering brings despair, callousness, and empty hope. We, as the children of God's kingdom, need to realize and take advantage of the power which comes through the fire of the sanctification process—a power which comes from God himself. "For the kingdom of God is not a matter of talk but of power" (1 Corinthians 4:20).

The Refining of the Soul

Humanistic living puts man's desire for comfort ahead of God's desire for our sanctification. We often forget the ironic blessing of suffering, because peace and safety become our substitute god. But Paul puts our mission in focus when he says, "For it has been granted to you on behalf of Christ not only to believe on him, but also to suffer for him" (Philippians 1:29).

We habitually want to be secure and safe—comfortable rather than transformed into the image of Jesus Christ (2 Corinthians 3:18). Spiritual transformation usually comes through refinement in this world, and in Scripture it is likened to fire (Isaiah 48:10, 1 Peter 1:7). Better to be refined in the fire of this world than to burn in the everlasting fire, where there is apparently no refining any more. But each of us must go through either one fire or the other.

Actually, refinement by fire in this life is not that horrible. For Christ is at work in us to bring us closer to his image. That's spiritually good. Scripture tells us that it is time for the judgment of believers to begin now (1 Peter 4:17). This judgment takes place through a refinement process—a refining of the soul.

Our escape from the eternal fire which does not refine was none of our own doing. God himself paid the price for our redemption. Therefore, let us seek out the change God wants for our lives by facing the challenge of the trials which come our way. Paul describes the spiritually logical progression a believer goes through when he is being refined: "We rejoice in the hope of the glory of God. Not only so, but we also rejoice in our sufferings, because we know that suffering produces perseverance; perseverance, character; and character, hope" (Romans 5:2-4).

James, too, describes the spiritual growth which takes place in the lives of maturing Christians. He gives us a message of encouragement, telling us to have a positive frame of mind—confidence rather than discouragement. He tells us, "Consider it pure joy, my brothers, whenever you face trials of many kinds, because you know that the testing of your faith develops perseverance. Perseverance must finish its work so that you may be mature and complete, not lacking anything" (James 1:2-4). Confidence and perseverance give us the guts to get in the battle where inevitably there is suffering. Gradually we become changed into the likeness of Jesus Christ, and in this we give praise, glory, and honor to God.

Even in the midst of terrible trials we are encouraged to persevere in doing good. "So then, those who suffer according to God's will should commit themselves to their faithful Creator and continue to do good" (1 Peter 4:19).

Yes, God has equipped each of us to be a very practical part of his power in this world. My prayer is that you and I might ever more consistently live out the admonition of Paul's words: "Be on your guard; stand firm in the faith; be men of courage; be strong. Do everything in love" (1 Corinthians 16:13-14). How? Why? "For it is God who works in you to will and to act according to his good purpose" (Philippians 2:13).

Values Which Shape Our Lives

Our values and our strong desires are extremely powerful instruments for God's use in our lives. They are the motivators that lie subconsciously under the surface, sort of hiding, so we don't often see them. But they have great power in determining just about everything we do. The consistency in our lives comes from our convictions, our values, our strong desires, our attitudes about life (all of these terms I use interchangeably for the purpose of this teaching).

Our *deep-seated values* give consistency and determination to our lives. My mother was often ridiculed as a child because she was Jewish, and I sympathized with her deeply when I was told of those traumatic encounters. As a result, I now have a strong value for fairness. It is such a strong conviction in me that I am able to be fair even with my worst enemies.

When our values are righteous or godly, they help us to be more consistent Christians, because they operate in our lives even when we have our minds on other things. That is why Jesus was intent on teaching us principles rather than specific remedies for every situation. Before he died he could have written or dictated to an educated friend an encyclopedia of righteous behavior for practically all situations. Instead, it was Jesus' intent to teach us principles, such as "Seek first [God's] kingdom" (Matthew 6:33), "Do not worry about tomorrow" (Matthew 6:34), "It is more blessed to give than to receive" (Acts 20:35), and "The last will be first, and the first will be last" (Matthew 20:16).

Getting in touch with your *righteous desires* provides you with knowledge of some of the most powerful forces in your life. You may use an ability occasionally; a past experience in your life may help you serve the Lord once in a while; and you probably use your unique personality characteristics to serve God daily. But your desires *constantly* guide your selection of significant tasks for the Lord.

We have already discussed the fact that many of our strengths and weaknesses come from God. But what about our desires? God makes a promise which relates to the implantation of his desires in us: "Delight yourself in the Lord and he will give you the desires of your heart" (Psalm 37:4). It logically makes sense that God would give us only desires which are according to his will for our lives. He not only *fulfills* our heart's desires, but he gives us those desires in the first place!

The secret of acquiring godly desires is to delight more and more in the Lord. As you find your pleasure in him, he places his desires in you. As you recognize those desires, you can participate with God in fulfilling them. Because of the promise of Psalm 37:4, I feel that godly desires are directional signs pointing toward the ministries God has for each of us individually within the church.

Some of the exercises at the end of this chapter ask you to discover some of your own godly desires through values clarification exercises. These specifically designed exercises should bring out your godly convictions. Whenever your first impression in response to one of the exercise questions is inconsistent with your answer after you have thought about it long and seriously, then perhaps you have an internal civil war going on in the deciding of your values. The solution to that kind of battle is to study God's attributes until you can so delight in him that you wish to serve no one but him—not even yourself. Then you will experience the transformation of your convictions from selfish to godly ambitions.

When Jean and I lead a marriage workshop, we use a few of these values clarification questions to help husbands and wives more deeply understand one another. Since we know from Scripture that one of the primary ministries of a married person is to take care of his spouse, we consider it very important for each husband and wife to know some of the deep things about each other. To know the how and why of the answers to each of these questions has been a great help to Jean and me. It helped us significantly to know what we would each like to hear Jesus Christ compliment us on after we die.

Four years ago when Jean and I did these exercises, I learned that Jean wants the Lord to compliment her for being a good wife and mother, and that she wants this compliment above all others. Knowing this bit of information, I have determined to try in whatever way necessary to help her be the kind of righteous wife and mother she wants to be. When I see her slipping in certain ways, I give a tremendous amount of myself to get her back on track.

It also helped Jean to know that the compliment I want most to hear from the Lord is, "You've been kind to the poor." Not only did she learn something deep from my heart, but we solved a disagreement about where we would spend a considerable portion of our tithe.

In a similar way, your answers to the exercise questions should point you in the direction God is leading you in the church. When your answers are somewhat repetitive, you will see evidence of strong desires. To the degree that you delight in the Lord, you can trust that those desires are God's calling to you for specific ministry in a certain area—a ministry matched to your abilities, life circumstances, and personality characteristics.

Spiritual Gifts: A Bonus From God

When we consider our strengths, values, and desires, we should also consider the supernatural abilities that the Holy Spirit places in us. Scripture teaches us that there are spiritual gifts given to us in order that God's supernatural power may flow through us for the edification and building up of the body of Christ (Romans 12 and 1 Corinthians 12). Many of us believe that these spiritual gifts are not given for our individual good but for the common good of the whole church. In any event, spiritual gifts can enhance our godly self-respect because they confirm that God is using us for his work.

There is some disagreement about the number of gifts that exist. However, if you see an ability occurring in you which is clearly from God, then don't bother yourself with what it's called. Call it anything, but realize that the Holy Spirit has empowered you with a gift to give to others.

With the spiritual gifts of exhortation and wisdom, the Holy Spirit augments my natural ability with supernatural ability. When I stop to help someone, my ability to provide counsel is supplemented by certain wisdom I've never even considered before. Such spontaneous, insightful responses to people tend to encourage and exhort them. And so I see a combination of a natural talent which has been improved by study (counseling) meshed together with God's supernatural provisions for the particular person to whom I am speaking (wisdom and exhortation).

As I counsel, I have that thrilling experience of working together with the Lord, using the abilities and gifts he has implanted in me. The more I counsel, the more I am convinced that God and I are doing it together—and it's a thrilling kind of harmony to experience! We need more of this kind of *teamwork with God*. The thrill of such an experience can be great enough to counteract any depression we might struggle with in our lives.

Recycling the Junk in Our Lives

Your life is full of experiences God can use in order to work his purposes in the world through you. Your own experiences help you perceive the world in a unique and therefore extremely valuable way. Consequently, your values become uniquely expressed because of your different life experiences. For example, I perceive my value of fairness in a considerably racial way because of the rejection my mother felt as a Jew. Others with a strong conviction about what is right who come from different life experiences will perceive fairness with a different emphasis. The way we perceive a value affects the way we set forth that value. God gave each of us different life experiences to shape our values in preparation for specific tasks in service to him.

God is in the process of recycling the junk from our past. The trauma of my childhood is often useful to those clients who recognize that their background and their lives have not been nearly as traumatic as mine. Not that the contrast in itself serves to motivate them—but they are encouraged when they see that I am successfully able to cope with life.

In a similar way, my wife's somewhat sad experience of not being raised by her natural mother opened the door for a strong conviction, which eventually led to our foster daughter, Laura, being able to have two mothers without conflict. (Her natural mother eats dinner with us regularly.)

My wife and I can see, in those two examples, the garbage or trauma from both of our childhoods being used for the good of others. Thus we can both begin to look at the past in a new light. What was painful and seemingly valueless has become transformed—in our relationship with Jesus Christ—into more value than we could ever imagine, because it brings glory to God.

The past pain is worth it in light of the glory which is given to the One who saved us from the world of darkness, bringing us into his beautiful kingdom of light (Colossians 1:12-13). As the garbage of our lives is transformed into service to others, the painful memories disappear. Thus, what we remember are the victories God has worked in us and in others through the very tragedies of our past.

The patriarch Joseph serves as an example here. Sold by his brothers into slavery, persecuted by someone else's unfaithful wife, and betrayed by a fellow worker, Joseph was transformed from a protected little boy into a seasoned man of God. Joseph became consumed with concern for the people of Israel, as well as the heathen people upon whom God wanted to grant his grace and mercy in time of famine. And so Joseph became governor over Egypt, and was used by God to free not only the pagan Egyptians, but the starving Israelites as well. A significant recycling indeed!—Joseph's misery was transformed into a great deliverance for many people. (Joseph's story is told in Genesis 37, 39-50.)

One of the most mind-shaking passages in the Bible refers to God's redemptive work within our lives. "We know that in all things God works for the good of those who love him, who have been called according to his purpose. For those God foreknew he also predestined to be conformed to the likeness of his Son, that he might be the firstborn among many brothers" (Romans 8:28-29). What a promise this is! God is so infinitely creative that he can recycle—for our benefit—all of the junk in our lives.

Have you ever really considered how creative the Creator is?! Even when we sin and have to face the natural and spiritual consequences of that sin, God is still creative enough to take that sin and its consequences and turn them to our good. He can take the good things, the neutral things, the sins, and the trauma of our lives, and use them all for our own good!

With God's view of things, we can see the great potential in all the events of our lives, particularly the negative ones. Where God has not yet used our negative experiences for our benefit, we ought to move steadily toward the day when he will be able to use us so totally that then we will perpetually see his holy power working in our lives. In our sincere service to him, we should desire to see the transformation of all our trauma into his glory! By and by we will be resurrected into the pure glory of heaven to ultimately and eternally gain more than we ever lost—to rejoice forever, in spite of the sufferings we experience here and now on the earth!

I know many people who have had very ugly life experiences, but who have been able to turn those experiences into service for God in the building up of the body of Christ. I think of victims of incest who have gone on with righteous determination to break the pattern of incest in their family tree. They have gone on to counsel other incest victims, to help create laws against incest, and to be sensitively available when someone in the church suffers pain of a similar nature. In God's eyes, a battalion of incest-victim believers goes out every day to do mighty things in warfare against the evil one, Satan, who is so twisted that he perpetually goes out of his way to infest the human race with sexual abominations.

The mercy and comfort of God is passed on by his children, who help to heal the anguish of the suffering masses (2 Corinthians 1:3-5). The one who has faced the pain of a unique trial can share a unique comfort with those who face that same trial. When people who lose a loved one through suicide truly accept the deliverance of God, they are ready to be called into duty as a unique division in the army of God, staying up all night long, if necessary, with a suicidal friend. So do they raise many from the potentially dead.

Those who suffer incurable illnesses often utilize their

spiritual and emotional sensitivity in a unique way. They depend more on God on a daily basis than most people do. The agony and imminence of a terminal illness is valuable to them *if* they allow God to build patience and sensitivity into their lives. People who gain this kind of unique maturity are ready to take up the ministry of consolation, touching the lives of others who are in pain and distress.

Grow to Be Yourself

As we consider how God redeems and recycles the negative and painful events of our lives, we need to consider also the somewhat obvious fact that he redeems the positive events as well. It is easier for us to remember the traumatic times, for during those times our bodies were mobilized with either anger or fear against the trauma. Our memories record stronger impressions of those uncomfortable and traumatic events than of the neutral and pleasant ones. Remembering the positive things in our lives, therefore, is more of a struggle—one which requires the Lord's help and our perseverance.

If you keep a list of positive things you've done in your lifetime, adding to that list as things come to mind, then you will see indications of strengths which develop through your accomplishments and positive experiences. If you appreciate how positive things can lead to more positive things, then you will be more sensitive and aware of the contribution you can make in your marriage, your family, and your church. You will be in the unique position to say to yourself, "This is good, and I know that God can use it to make other things good." Such a positive attitude is contagious, especially when it is based on the transforming, redemptive work of God within our lives.

As you consider the process of spiritual maturity, or sanctification, you can learn a lot from observation. Look at the lives of those around you who are spiritually mature. Or look in the Bible. The apostle Paul encourages us to follow his example. The writer of Hebrews encourages us to follow the examples of the great heroes of the faith (Hebrews 11). And certainly we are to follow the perfect example of Jesus Christ.

A comparison of your life with that of a spiritual example is righteous only when it leads to appropriate goals, not when it leads to placing unrealistic expectations on people, including yourself. When you compare yourself with Jesus Christ, no pride is possible, for Jesus is always greater than we are.

In light of Galatians 6:4-5, which warns us not to proudly compare ourselves with others, you can take a long, hard look at yourself in light of all that God wants *you* to become. He wants you to grow to become yourself! And you can do this without comparing yourself with others. Sanctification recognizes that God is working in you to perfect you into the image of Jesus Christ; envy doesn't.

The Lord will probably use the example of many godly people to show you some areas of necessary change within yourself. But to covet or envy the righteousness of those people in order to be better than they are is surely folly and sin. On the other hand, to study and admire the righteousness of others in order to grow with them and spur them on to greater righteousness—not out of competition, but through mutual ministry—this is *godly* desire, not envy or covetousness. Such a godly perspective will give you an appropriate, objective respect for yourself which is between you and God, not between you and others.

If we could only grasp this idea that there is no room for competition and envy in the body of Christ, then we would understand that there is nothing about which to boast. The fact that you and I do certain things more excellently than some other people is inevitable. But our quick response should be, "Of course, it was my task! God assigned it to me and empowered me to do it!" At the same time we should recognize that there are many other areas in which our brothers and sisters are equipped to excel.

We need to be careful that we do not delude ourselves about

our spiritual growth. We should be growing simultaneously in both righteous self-confidence and humility. We can take a lesson in this area from the life of Solomon. Due to his strong desire to have wisdom, Solomon indeed gained wisdom from God. He became known as the wisest man in the world (1 Kings 3-4). But even with all of his wisdom, Solomon became spoiled and corrupt. He was not careful to control his gift of wisdom, for he foolishly acquired many women who worshiped idols—a total of seven hundred wives and three hundred concubines. His wives led him to worship other gods, a spiritual evil which went far beyond the life of Solomon alone. For the folly of this once wise man led to gross idolatry among the people of God (1 Kings 11).

We need to remember that in a sense our strengths and weaknesses are not our own because *we* are not our own (1 Corinthians 6:19-20). We live in a day and age when people value the acquisition of something for its own sake. Knowledge and wisdom become a selfish end rather than a righteous means. The Bible cautions that "Knowledge puffs up, but love builds up" (1 Corinthians 8:1). God wants us to see that learning for any other sake than serving and glorifying him is meaningless and potentially destructive, as we observed in the case of Solomon. Our Lord wants us to see that *love* is the means for building up others as well as ourselves. Both love and wisdom are gifts from God—righteous means to *his* righteous ends.

Since God has a limited number of tasks for each of us to do, it is wise to limit our learning to those areas of appointed assignments. Let us not hop from one self-enhancement program to another, or from one type of church ministry to another. We need rather to be concerned with enhancing God's work in the world through the significant but limited assets he has given us. God himself challenges us to go through the fire of life itself in order to be refined for *his purposes*. Such a spiritual growth process will inevitably build up our sense of righteous self-confidence, because we will know that we are inside the will of God.

Work sheet instructions for: "My God-Inspired Desires"
In this section, we are dealing with values clarification exercises, which will hopefully give you an idea of your values and strong convictions. You are asked to complete a thought in each exercise. Try to be specific. There are no exclusively right answers to these values clarification questions. Essentially we are attempting to find out how God might be speaking to you about what is important, or, more specifically, about what he wants you to consider important, so that you might become involved in a ministry in that area.

Exercise One
In exercise or question one, you are not being asked for the *only* compliment that you would like to hear, but rather for the one you would want to hear more than any others. Try to be specific so that you can discover your God-inspired desires. For what reason would Jesus say to you, "Well done, good and faithful servant"? (Matthew 25:14-30). It will probably be helpful to answer this question in terms of a type of work for the Lord, rather than a description of your walk with the Lord. We should desire God's approval not to boost our own egos, but to be reassured that we have helped to effectively do his work.

Exercise Two
In exercise two, you are asked how you would spend your precious, last portion of time if you knew you were dying. To prepare yourself to answer this one, why not try a little imagery? Close your eyes and imagine a meeting with your doctor, in which he states that you definitely have no more than five years to live. Imagine yourself feeling devastated and disappointed at first, but then working this through to the point where you are feeling excited about going to be with the Lord. When you can imagine yourself accepting that you have just five years to live, then open your eyes and complete the statement, "If I had the talent, the courage, and only five years to live, what would I do in the church?"

Exercise Three

In exercise three of the values clarification exercises, you are trying to uncover what God might have inspired you to desire for the church. Again, it might help if you close your eyes and imagine actually sitting there *alone* with the Lord. Take your time and think this through carefully. You might want to write down ideas that come to your mind right away and then evaluate which three you feel are most important to you.

Please answer this from your own perspective, trying not to give pat Christian answers. God will probably lead everybody to fill this question out differently. This is as it should be, since the church has many needs. Furthermore, God does not call all people to the same ministries.

Exercise Four

In exercise four, you are to complete the statement: "I wish someone in my church would...." Try to list three things you wish other people would do. Your responses here may very likely be an indication of what God wants *you* to do, unless you are convinced that you do not have the resources in either talent or time.

Exercise Five

In exercise five, it is important to be specific. If you are planning to give your imaginary money to the church budget, then write down what you would specifically want it to be spent for. Some people would want to spread the money among many favorite projects, both in and outside the local church. This exercise is designed to help you identify in yet one more way those things in the overall work of the church which are most important to you because God placed them on your heart.

You are not making any theological decisions here regarding what is most important in the work of the church. For example, some would spend no money for missions and yet readily agree that missions is one of the most critical works of the church. But because the Lord has placed upon them another burden, they would give their money to some other work of the church instead of missions, trusting that others would be called by the Lord to give their money to missions. Please do not worry about giving the "right" answers or standard Christian answers. Dig deeply and spend that money wisely in the way that you feel the Lord would tell you to spend it.

Taking an Overall View

After you have completed this first page, entitled "My God-Inspired Desires," you should have a better idea concerning the direction of ministry in which God wants to lead you. Your desires can be greatly used in the work of the Lord. Without strong desires, I suspect not very much would get done in the work of the church.

As you analyze your answers to these values clarification exercises, take note of the areas you repeatedly make reference to. Look for patterns of repetition. If the area of missions keeps showing up, then perhaps you need to ask yourself if you're being called to more involvement in missions, as a missionary, as a member of the missions committee of your church, or maybe as a regional representative to appeal for funds for missionary support. Go through this sheet on God-inspired desires and circle those things which are common among your answers. Those areas you circle are very likely God's leading for your area of ministry.

The first item, the compliment you would most like to hear from the Lord after your death, is extremely important. Pursuit of that compliment, provided it is a godly pursuit, should consume the energies of your life between now and when you die. You should tell others around you how important it is, so that they might help you in that area. It may not be your major ministry at this time. But, since it is so very important to you, you should definitely lay plans to start working on the area in which you want to greatly please God. All too often we allow the "urgent" to crowd out the really important. But don't let this happen in your life.

My God-Inspired Desires

1. After I die, when I stand before Jesus Christ for the first time, the compliment I most want to hear is . . .

   _____

   _____

2. If I had the talent, the courage, and only five years to live, what would I do in the church?

   _____

   _____

   _____

3. If Jesus were to visit me tonight and promise to grant me three wishes for the church, I would wish for . . .

   _____

   _____

   _____

4. I wish someone in my church would . . .

   _____

   _____

   _____

5. If I were to inherit one million dollars, how would I distribute the tithe? (10% would be $100,000.)

   _____

   _____

Work sheet instructions for: "My God-Redeemable Life Experiences"

On this second work sheet, you need to write down life experiences God has given you in order to prepare you for particular kinds of ministry. Please consider carefully Romans 8:28, which is listed at the top of the work sheet.

God may not have *designed* sinful experiences, but he did allow them. He can now creatively use them for your own good and for his work in the world. Since God has been so sovereign as to allow good and bad experiences, you should be aware of those experiences, so that you can extract some positive value from them in your ministry.

In the first section, write down your significant childhood experiences, both positive and negative. It is often much easier to remember the negatives. However, we should rest in the Scriptures which teach that we can grow a great deal from our trials. But certainly our positive experiences are important, too, even though they are sometimes more difficult to recall.

In the second section, list your significant accomplishments of the past. Do not compare your accomplishments with those of other people, but try to think of eight of the most significant things you have done. Ask the Holy Spirit to bring to your mind those events which God counts as significant.

Maybe you have planned a large banquet, or maybe you led a social program to help the poor. Whatever those significant accomplishments might be, list them—God might need those skills some time in the future. Knowing what you have done well will help you to recognize the ways in which God is asking you to serve.

Perhaps there are some important experiences which don't fit into either of the first two categories. Four spaces are given for miscellaneous important experiences; please list them there.

God has been working in your life to give you certain characteristics. He has given you some things genetically (through heredity) and he has also allowed certain life experiences to further mold your personality. The fifteen spaces here in this fourth section are for those fifteen items you starred on the work sheet at the end of Chapter Seven, entitled "My God-Given Characteristics." Transfer those fifteen starred items to the bottom of this work sheet under the title, "My God-Molded Personality Traits."

My God-Redeemable Life Experiences

> We know that in all things God works for the good of those who love him, who have been called according to his purpose. (Romans 8:28)

Significant Childhood Experiences, Both Positive and Negative

1) _____   4) _____
   _____   _____

2) _____   5) _____
   _____   _____

3) _____   6) _____
   _____   _____

Significant Accomplishments of the Past

1) _____   3) _____
   _____   _____

2) _____   4) _____
   _____   _____

5) _____   7) _____

_____   _____

6) _____   8) _____

_____   _____

Miscellaneous Important Experiences

1) _____   3) _____

_____   _____

2) _____   4) _____

_____   _____

My God-Molded Personality Traits

1) _____   9) _____

2) _____   10) _____

3) _____   11) _____

4) _____   12) _____

5) _____   13) _____

6) _____   14) _____

7) _____   15) _____

8) _____

11

STEP SIX: DECLARING WAR ON YOUR SINS

Count yourselves dead to sin but alive to God in Christ Jesus. Therefore do not let sin reign in your mortal body so that you obey its evil desires. Do not offer the parts of your body to sin, as instruments of wickedness, but rather offer yourselves to God, as those who have been brought from death to life; and offer the parts of your body to him as instruments of righteousness.

Romans 6:11-13

A white flag of surrender should be raised only when a battle is clearly lost. But the spiritual warfare between God and Satan has already been decided, and the people of God are on the winning side because of the death and resurrection of Jesus Christ. Yet Satan has refused to raise a white flag. He continues to fight on. But we know, as he knows, that he is doomed to defeat.

Why is it, then, that many of the people of God are not fighting a victorious battle against sin in their lives? Don't we have the upper hand in the battle against the forces of evil? Isn't the omnipotent God fighting on our side, providing us with all the best spiritual weaponry? Why, then, have many of the soldiers of God raised the white flag of surrender to sin in their lives?

People who habitually give in to sin live defeated lives–spiritually, emotionally, psychologically, and often physically. They have no sense of self-respect because they realize they are dishonoring themselves daily through the pollution of deliberate sin. But the battle does not need to be abandoned by any child of God. Victory is still within sight, even for the most desperate of sinners.

In step six we want to take a good look at the Christian's personal battle against sin. Someone who is truly engaged in the spiritual battle against sin and evil will not have a self-defeated attitude. A dedicated Christian will be armed with a godly confidence that God is supplying all the vital armaments for battle against the spiritual foe. Each one of us should take a look in the spiritual mirror to see how devoted we really are in our battle against sin.

Warfare Can Be Exhilarating

A successful battle against personal sin is critical to the development of a godly self-respect. Since we are so far from being like Jesus Christ, each of us has many sins to battle in the process of becoming conformed to the image of our Lord and Savior. Therefore, a godly self-respect cannot be based on a total absence of sin in our lives. But it can and should be reinforced by progressive victories against personal sins.

The apostle John warned that it is a serious error to say we have no sin in our lives (1 John 1:8-10). We would do well to comprehend that we fall *far* short of the glory of God, not just a little short. The prophet Isaiah cried out that even our *righteousness* is like a soiled rag when compared with the righteousness of God (Isaiah 64:6). Thus it appears obvious that we are facing a lifelong battle with personal sin.

But that battle should be something we look forward to rather than something we dread. Far too many people are so ashamed of the sin in their lives that they avoid even thinking about it. As a result, they are quite ineffective in putting an end to their personal sins. Since we will be involved in battling personal sin all of our lives, and since this battle is a part of the process of becoming like Jesus Christ, it can, in fact, be an exhilarating experience.

Imagine how different it would be if, when we woke up in the morning, we were excited about the prospect of living the day in a dedicated battle to overcome personal sins. We would wake up with a sense of anticipation and excitement instead of a feeling of defeat. The joy of battle, together with the sustaining presence of God, would carry us on to a reaffirming sense of victory in our lives.

Each of us has certain major sins which hold back our godly self-respect. The sins differ from person to person. But each one of us has a dirty closet. If we do not yet know what's in the dirty closet, we can open our lives to the scrutiny of the Spirit of God and the Scriptures to find out. As we admit our sinfulness to God in obedience to Scripture (1 John 1:8-10), God accordingly makes us aware of certain sins in our lives. He wants us to recognize those sins, confess them, and seek a changed life through *repentance*—turning away from those sins.

After we eliminate the undermining influence of these sins, we are more inclined to follow the spiritual growth process described by Paul: "We, who with unveiled faces all reflect the Lord's glory, are being transformed into his likeness with ever-increasing glory, which comes from the Lord, who is the Spirit" (2 Corinthians 3:18).

But how can we be transformed when we wear the veil of sin? We must shed this unrighteous veil and yield to the righteous power of God. God is working a continual process of sanctification in our lives. The Holy Spirit, who lives within us, is at work toward certain purposes. This means that at any particular point in time, the sins that God is convicting us of are the sins he expects us to battle. It is only natural that our refusal to thus engage in battle robs us of a godly self-respect.

For example, during the time that I am writing this chapter God is convicting me of the sin of not responding in a godly fashion to untrue accusations. When I was growing up, I was conditioned to believe that anything that goes wrong must be my fault. I grew up constantly defending myself in an effort to preserve some self-love and acceptance. Now when I am accused or judged unjustly, I still panic sometimes. By the help of God I have overcome a great deal of defensiveness and the reaction of striking back. But at times I still have internal anger and ungodly withdrawal when people accuse me incorrectly.

Since I recognize this sin, I sincerely confess it to God and receive forgiveness from him. Thus even in my sin life I work in partnership with God. As part of my fight against this sin, I am meditating on Scriptures which deal with the many times Jesus was accused falsely. As I study his reactions to false accusations, I pray for the power to act more like him. Rather than selfishly withdrawing to be protected from false accusation, I am learning how to move out in the spirit of wisdom and reconciliation.

This is not an easy change for me. My love for God, more than any self-seeking pragmatic reason, drives me to succeed in this major battle of my life. I see myself as a knight going out daily to battle the dragons of sin. I want to please the King by fighting the dragons with courage and perseverance, wearing the full armor of God (Ephesians 6:10-18).

The Warning Signal of Guilt

Many people do not understand the role of *guilt* in God's plan. Guilt is a universal feeling. But what does it mean? It appears to be a gift from God—both a signal and a motivating force for change.

Negative feelings usually signal that something is going wrong, whereas positive feelings usually signal that something is going right. All too often we fail to pay attention to either of these signals because we have been taught to ignore our feelings or to conclude that feelings are categorically bad, especially the negative ones. For example, most of us will have a primary feeling that comes into our awareness at certain times to signal that something is going wrong. If we can tune into that feeling early when it is less intense, we can then trace back to the cause of the feeling and identify problems while they are still small and uncomplicated.

Some feelings can perpetually energize us to solve problems and get things done. Other feelings have served their purpose once they have signaled something to us. Guilt is one of the latter, having run its course after it clearly signals to us that there is sin in our lives.

Guilt is a valuable signal of sin only when it comes from God through the message of Scripture, through godly counsel, or through the conviction of the Holy Spirit. There is another kind of guilt—the worldly variety—which originates solely from the expectations of others. For example, sometimes we feel guilty when we witness to unbelievers. But the guilt we feel when someone is nervous while we explain our faith is a feeling which does not emanate from God. It is, in fact, a feeling of guilt which should basically be ignored.

When you feel guilt, you can usually trace it back to its source, thus analyzing the real problem. When the guilt comes from an ungodly source or it is unconfirmed by Bible teaching, you should probably take it with a grain of salt, or at least minimize its impact. When the guilt comes from God, you can consider it a blessing, thus thanking him for pointing out an impurity in your life.

Guilt can help us see those areas of our lives which God wants us to perfect to righteousness in Christ. It is not a feeling to hang on to after it has been utilized in this function of identification of sin. The next logical step is not a period of self-flagellation with the whip of guilt, but rather an act of repentance, which is a decision of the will—not forced by the feeling of guilt, but rather triggered by grateful love for the Lord.

Throughout Scripture we are told to hate sin. But Scripture does not tell us to hate the sinner. Hatred, therefore, can be a righteous feeling only when directed at sin, not at people. Once we have discarded our guilt through confession of the sin pointed out by that guilt, then we should put into action our love for God and hatred for sin by turning away from our sin. Our disgust with sin—but not with ourselves or other people—can powerfully motivate us to make a decision for repentance, which brings us always closer to God and the kind of righteous self-respect befitting a soldier of God.

Many secular psychotherapists have mistakenly identified guilt as *the* basic problem of mankind—a feeling which should be eradicated from life. Unfortunately, they are somewhat accurate in that our primary motivation to change should not be guilt. (It should actually be our love for God.) They go too far, of course, in their total dismissal of guilt. But Christians should not seek to be guilt-ridden in order to take the opposite stand from that of secular psychologists. For when guilt is our primary feeling, we can be assured only of depression, not of victory.

The Key to the Metamorphosis
The Bible points out clearly that the motivating force for obedience and holiness in our lives must be our love for Jesus Christ (John 14:21). Love for God, not guilt about sins, is the power we should marshal in order to battle against our personal sins. Throughout much of the Old Testament, we see that Israel's disobedience was a natural result of her lost love for God. When the people turned to the love of idols, then sin ran rampant among their ranks.

Herein lies the basic problem of non-victorious living in evangelical Christians of America: we have chosen the wrong weapon with which to battle personal sin. We have chosen guilt, instead of love and obedience to God, as the way to shape up our lives. How sad is this spiritual error. For the more positive feeling of *love* can bring on the powerful results we seek.

Our motivation for fighting sin should be our love for God, as expressed in *obedience* to him. When we become motivated to change ourselves in order to avoid guilt or to be more personally successful, then we are just complicating our sin with more sin. Many people within the church do not obey God as an expression of love, but rather out of fear of punishment or the desire to achieve "Christian success." This warped perspective removes something valuable from the beneficial, loving relationship we should all be having with the God of the universe through his Son, Jesus Christ.

We water down salvation itself when we regard a personal

relationship with God as less important than a place in heaven. While it is true that Scripture holds out the promise of a mansion in God's heavenly kingdom, the apostle Paul writes that *nothing* surpasses the greatness of knowing God personally (Philippians 3:8). Knowing God personally and having a relationship with him must be the main attraction. We Christians are to glory in our relationship with God. Dwelling in a mansion is certainly secondary to having a personal relationship with the Benefactor of that mansion.

When the rewards and benefits of being a King's son outweigh the importance of a loving relationship with the King, then it is quite natural to fear his judgment and to use that fear to eradicate sin from one's life. But God does not want us to deal with our sins primarily out of fear. He wants us to act out of love. This alone will bring on the true metamorphosis.

You have probably seen in yourself and in many of your friends the crippling effect of guilt. Such guilt is not liberating—it is condemning. It extends too far. For although the kind of guilt which acts as a signal to point out personal sin can be quite penetrating, nevertheless it does not last forever. It points out sin and truly gets our attention. But then, after confession, we should no longer hang on to that guilt, hoping that it will somehow cause us to change (1 John 1:9). While that may work with some of our smaller sins, I have rarely seen it work effectively in getting rid of the more established sins in a person's life. For generally one's overly extended guilt does not supply enough motivation to bring on change. Eventually depression sets in and robs the person of the energy and optimism necessary to battle that personal sin.

Bad feelings about self merely keep sin in control at best. Sin is not destroyed by guilt alone. For the fact is that each time sin rears its ugly head again, more discouragement comes, until ultimately the person gives up any serious attempt to control that sin.

An even more critical mistake is the sinful attempt to change one's life in order to avoid guilt. Such a focus is as humanistic as doing what feels good or seems right, without considering God. If one's central motivation to change is to get rid of guilt or to avoid guilt, he is manifesting love for self, not love for God. Instead, we should desire to change *because* we love God. It is obvious that hanging on to guilt after confession of sin is a very great sin in itself. In a way, it is a slap in God's face because it indicates that our love for him is of a lesser priority than some weak, manipulative guilt utilized to achieve personal growth.

Dumping the Guilty Conscience

The Bible tells us that the death of Christ can deliver us from a guilty conscience. "How much more, then, will the blood of Christ, who through the eternal Spirit offered himself unblemished to God, cleanse our consciences from acts that lead to death, so that we may serve the living God!" (Hebrews 9:14).

Thus we are urged to "draw near to God with a sincere heart in full assurance of faith, having our hearts sprinkled to cleanse us from a guilty conscience . . ." (Hebrews 10:22). When we hang on to our guilt after we have asked for forgiveness with a sincere heart, then our confidence wanes and we violate the teaching of Scripture: "Do not throw away your confidence; it will be richly rewarded" (Hebrews 10:35).

Habitual sin tears away at one's self-respect. If you belong to Christ, then you have the Holy Spirit dwelling inside. Thus there is no way to practice sin repeatedly without losing respect for yourself. You can attempt to throw off concern for morality, but deep down inside you will be reminded that you are not living up to all you can be. Practiced sin will continually bring a barrage of guilt messages from the Lord, which are intended to lead you to turn to him in confession and repentance.

If you habitually sin, you will be bombarded with problems. God will sharply prod you with convicting arrows of guilt. In this way your own conscience will tell you that you are out of harmony with spiritual standards, and the natural consequences of sin will eventually cause havoc in your life.

The answer to habitual sin is habitual battle against sin. Every believer needs this spiritually militant attitude to fully participate in the process whereby God works in us to perfect us in holiness. To fully enjoy the sanctification process is to discover deliverance from the practice of sin. The incongruity of practicing sin and battling it at the same time should cause us to open our eyes to the spiritual games we may be playing. One needs to be relatively consistent in life. We either practice sin or practice battling against sin. Only one of these attitudes will prevail.

The Spiritual Guts to Fight

For our own well-being, we should utilize guilt as a signal of sin, as God intends it to be used. After we have confessed our sins and repented, then we can discard our guilt and begin to enjoy a new battle against other personal sins. As in any battle, defeats which occur in minor skirmishes are relatively insignificant as long as the larger battle is won. So we should look less at each little personal complication, instead letting the thrill of ultimate victory consume us. Such a righteous desire should overcome our tendency to avoid taking action for fear of temporary failures.

The sins most people deal with are not simple. Furthermore, Satan is no dummy. Thus, saying *No* to big temptations in our lives is quite difficult, and all too often we just give up. But we need to begin to accept the fact that, yes, we have lost some of our battles against sin. But minor losses are simply part of the nature of war. All the more reason not to give up, but to renew our strength in the Lord and to resume the battle until we are victorious!

And why not enjoy this process? No one likes to lose a battle, but, like the football team which is behind at half time, we must come back stronger and even more determined to win. Even though our discouragement sometimes fights against us, God is on our side and the victory has been promised. You must always remember that "the one who is in you is greater than the one who is in the world" (1 John 4:4).

We have already seen that the biggest weapon we have against sin is our love for God. If your love is an all-consuming love, then your mind and body will be mobilized to obedience. To be sure, sin might creep in. But if you adopt the attitude I am suggesting, then when sin does come to your mind you will shout, "Hurray!" For the enemy has then been spotted, and actions can thus be taken to destroy that personal sin which God has shown to you through his gift of revelation. After you see the nature of your sin, then you have the knowledge, so try to have the spiritual guts as well to fight against your own spiritual cancer.

There are other weapons we can use to battle sin in our lives. If we use the primary motivation of love for God, then we can use the additional weapons of prayer, Bible study, and planned actions.

Through *prayer*, we can ask God to reveal our sins to us to protect us from temptation, and to supervise our lives with his power.

The Bible contains God's written instructions to help us identify personal sin. Our study of Scripture is vitally important. It is through Bible study that our prayers for discovery of personal sin are often answered. It is also through Bible study that we learn of the appropriate godly attitudes and actions required of sinners who want to successfully battle ungodliness in their lives.

Finally, it is in *planned actions* that we exercise our wills in an intelligent fashion to arrange the strategic victory. God has given us the power to reason, and he expects us to use that power to plan a strategy against our sins.

Some people recommend a passive approach to sin based on Ephesians 4:22-24. They advise, "Put off the old self and put on the new self," as if putting off and putting on were simple, passive processes. This overly simplistic strategy, as in the formula "Let go and let God," has success in certain circumstances, but often falls short when the battle is against Satan's cleverness and the more tenacious sins in our lives.

I do see "Put off the old self" as a valid exhortation. But it requires great effort to understand the enemy, as well as the "old self"—its motivations and causes. Only when we have this understanding do we know which paths to take and which to avoid in order not only to survive the battle, but also to gain the victory.

Thus, armed with love for our Lord Jesus Christ, we seek knowledge of our personal sins. Once we understand the patterns of our thinking and acting which lead to the committing of our sins, we can lay a strategic plan to overcome them. Eventually we can become strong enough to confront the sin face-to-face and come out victorious, following the example of Jesus Christ. For he was victorious over all temptation and promised us that there is no temptation which can automatically overcome us (1 Corinthians 10:13).

THE WEAPON OF PRAYER

Prayer is a vital element in the seeking out and destroying of personal sin. If you're going to adopt the attitude of a warrior seeking to find the flaws in his battle skills in order to more proficiently slay dragons for his King, then I would suggest that you meditate on both the hope you have in Jesus Christ and also on the most effective way to battle your sins. Then aggressively pray to have your major sins revealed to you at this time in your life so you might do battle and know the joy of victory. Pray that you will always remember that God is on your side, for battling personal sin is not an individual effort, but a team effort with God.

Pray also that you will be aware of God's acceptance when you are faced with the knowledge of your personal sins. Ask him to remind you of the verse which states the spiritual fact that "while we were still sinners, Christ died for us" (Romans 5:8). Ask God for an attitude of self-acceptance which allows you to say to yourself, "Of course I have sins in my life. That is why I need a Savior. I want to find out what my sins are so that I can eliminate them from my life and become more like Jesus Christ."

If you keep this kind of positive perspective, then the repulsion at the revealing of your sin will not cause you to lose heart or to be overly ashamed. And so you will still be able to approach with boldness the throne of the King and seek his mercy (Hebrews 4:16). God's grace will then help you in your time of need.

Finally, you need to pray that when you see a new sin in your life, you will remain sensible, immediately seeking a spiritual remedy. By confessing your sin, you allow God to take away the load of your guilt, replacing it with his lighter yoke of repentance, a yoke he helps you carry.

THE WEAPON OF BIBLE STUDY

A systematic *study of Scripture* is also instrumental in finding the hidden strongholds of personal sin. Avoid studying only your favorite passages. The whole counsel of God will more fully reveal to you the recesses of your life where sinfulness lurks, subtly attacking your godly self-respect. Therefore, if you are going to ferret out your personal sins, if you are going to aggressively pursue the enemy, do it joyfully and do it through a complete study of Scripture.

Many of the sins that will be revealed to you will be easy to overcome. Your decisions for repentance will often lead to automatic responses in your life. Victory will come easily in these minor skirmishes with sin. Nevertheless, as small as these sins might appear to be, each victory will bring you closer to the glorious image of Jesus Christ.

But when you study passages of Scripture which you consider unfamiliar and uninspiring, you may find that therein lies a revelation of your deeper sins, where terrible spiritual dragons have control. The small victories are certainly rewarding, but it is in the slaying of those large, menacing monstrosities of greater sinfulness that you will become more confident, able to serve, and prepared for greater responsibilities for the Lord. When the large dragons are defeated, then the King can send you out on more difficult missions, perhaps to kill even larger dragons.

THE WEAPON OF PLANNED ACTIONS

God gave you the ability to reason. It is his design and desire for you to use your intelligence. There are very logical solutions to many of our sins—they are not some kind of abstract, spiritual mysteries. So many of our sins are habitually triggered by certain kinds of events, thoughts, and personal reactions. When we understand what triggers a particular sin, then we can go to the cause and lay a plan of attack for victory.

Planned actions are important in almost any area of life. For example, many people spend money in an ungodly fashion. Whether they buy unnecessary, extravagant things or get hopelessly in debt, they nevertheless handle their money in an unrighteous way. This kind of irresponsible purchasing is often stimulated by something within, such as feelings of worthlessness, personal anxiety, uncomfortable stress, low self-image, love for things (materialism), etc. But whatever the case, a plan of action is desperately needed.

Each individual sin calls for a different plan of action, a different topical study of the Scriptures, and a different decision of repentance. So if you are dealing with the sin of overspending, then you need a different strategy than you would use to deal with an unforgiving attitude. Sometimes you opt for a victory in a skirmish rather than victory in a major battle. In a skirmish you are discarding just one of the mutated expressions of the old self; in a major battle you can eliminate a whole complex of related sins at one time.

How much better it is to see ourselves as God sees us: as valuable people who do not need to have a lot of material things to make us important or worthwhile. When we take on God's objective view of things, then our service to the Lord and our relationships with people will be more fulfilling and "things" will have much less meaning. And if it's undue stress in our lives that causes us to go to the shopping mall in order to buy, then we should plan our lives so that we experience less stress, so that we do not turn to material things rather than to God in our anxiety. I hope you see that attacking the specific cause of a sin can remove an entire network of sins in your life. But specific causes usually call for specific plans of action.

After a sin is revealed to you and you have confessed it, make the brave decision to live your life *God's* way. Pray that God will constantly reveal your personal sins to you and activate his power in your life. Then study the Scriptures to discover some of your other sins and the right ways to react to them. Also plan logical actions which will not only bring you to an avoidance of particular sins in your life, but which will also gradually bring you closer to Jesus Christ. Do not go out of your way to avoid dealing with your sins, but rather face them squarely, denying yourself obedience to sin, but committing yourself to obedience to God as a dedicated warrior in his service.

In the Trenches With Your Friends
You need not fight your battles alone against sin. God gave you brothers and sisters—they can help you in your battles. He wants you to confess your sins to them so that they will be able to help you (James 5:16). True brothers and sisters will not publicly humiliate you, but they will help bear your burden by encouraging you and joining in your spiritual struggle.

None of us is in an individual warfare. We are uniquely bound together in the church so that through the strengths of each other we might be victorious. Together we can successfully navigate through the various trials of life. Most trials and temptations should be confronted with a unity of power in the church, not with the lonely challenge of the individual believer. Paul was addressing the collective body of the church when he said, "No temptation has seized you except what is common to man. And God is faithful; he will not let you be tempted beyond what you can bear. But when you are tempted, he will also provide a way out so that you can stand up under it" (1 Corinthians 10:13).

Godly fellowship is a critical factor in success over temptation. Rarely does a soldier who is wounded fail to call for help. No Christian should fail, for fear of humiliation, to seek help from a trusted Christian friend. For a true friend will hear our confession, accept us (Romans 15:7), and encourage us with godly advice. He will gladly join us in the trenches, and we will thus fight the battle together.

There is a general tendency in fallen man to hide sin. Even Adam and Eve tried to hide their sin from God (Genesis 3:8). Unfortunately, exposing our sins by confessing to one another and by asking for help is very difficult to do. It goes against our fallen nature. But God wants us to be delivered from our fallen nature. He wants us to share even the dregs of our lives with each other. But in Western society there is an ungodly tendency to elevate self-sufficiency, which makes it difficult to share our troubles and faults with others.

But the Bible refers to the ideal fellowship we are to have in the church. As the people of God, we are to be *interdependent*—accepting the fact that we all err and reaching out to each other to help in our diverse battles with sin. If we could make some significant progress in the church in this area, it would be a real blessing!

Imagine having a few friends with whom you could have this kind of mutual, give-and-take relationship. You could call them up at any time and say to them, "I'm sinning again and I need your help," or "I'm just about to yield to a temptation, so I'd like you to come over and talk," or "I'm putting myself down again, feeling terrible about myself, and I need your help." Just to be able to say "I'm sinning and I need your help" would create a relationship of accountability that would bring victory over many sins without nearly the struggle you would have all by yourself. When you get to those stubborn, longstanding sins, you might not be able to fight it alone; you might just need a good friend to minister God's help and strength to you.

There are times when my creativity can be used by God. There are other times when my creativity is like a millstone around my neck, because I lose sight of God's purpose for that creativity and load myself down with all kinds of creative projects. Those who are not so inventively inclined should be content in that, for perhaps God wanted a bit more stability in their lives in order that they might serve him in yet a different way.

One of the most persistent sins stemming from my creative energy is that I get overextended. I take on too many projects. But another result is that I get unrighteously angry in my frustration after I have overextended myself. That irritation may not come out directly, although I do become less sensitive, more businesslike, and sometimes shamefully curt.

I sometimes get angry at God for a situation I have created myself. In this particular area of my life, I definitely need friends to whom I can go for help and counsel. I need the kind of friends who do not have the same kinds of problems that I am trying to solve, although sometimes it helps to hear someone else's empirically proven, *righteous* way of handling the same kind of sin.

If I am concerned enough to try to live a godly life and to respect myself because I live a godly life, then I need to avail myself of the help God gives me through my fellow Christians. My brothers and sisters in Christ are one of the many resources helping me to live a righteous life. God gave me the Holy Spirit, the Bible, prayer, my wife and family, my elders and pastors, and *you*—my brothers and sisters. I hope you, too, will know the joy of the healing fellowship of the body of Christ.

We All Need to Change

While your guilt should lead you to the confession of your sin, your love for God should lead you to a decision of repentance. *Repent-*

ance is a changing of your mind and your actions about something. It involves more than regret and sorrow and confession. It goes beyond your emotions and thoughts to the perspective of God himself—the way he sees things and the way he wants things.

Your repentance has much more power when you have truly understood, as well as you can, the mind of God. When you see the world as *he* sees it, then repentance becomes a more natural decision. Such a decision is not superficial, but substantial. It will change your self-identity—the way you think about yourself. And it will change the way you act, because you will naturally resist acting in ways which are not consistent with your self-identity. As you reorient your ways of perceiving and understanding your own life, the resultant change of your mind and heart will affect your lifestyle greatly (Romans 12:1-2).

In true repentance, your *will* is necessarily engaged. If you are not truly *committed* to change, then your behavior, thoughts, and feelings will not change. We should seek the kind of repentance that signifies an all-consuming change. Legalistic obedience is no substitute for a transformed life. The only proper motivation for obedience, as Jesus pointed out, is *love for him*. He said, "Whoever has my commands and obeys them, he is the one who loves me" (John 14:21).

A complete repentance will eliminate many of the habitual sins which we are not yet aware of. For when we begin to think God's way, with a self-identity in harmony with his plan for us, then we will change many things about our behavior. For example, if, through the identification of a particular sin, you assertively wage a battle against materialism as your way of life, then you will eradicate not only the cause of the sin which you identified, but many other related sins as well. Perhaps your behavior will change in a very general way. You may vote differently. You may decide to leave a high-paying job to answer God's call to a full-time ministry. Or you may more freely and cheerfully give to the poor.

At any rate, once you are delivered from the grip of ungodly materialism, you will be changed in many ways—ways you were perhaps not conscious of before. And thus you will be a little bit closer to the image of Jesus Christ. In addition, these broad changes would probably generate many more Christlike decisions, attitudes, and behaviors. The momentum of a victory over sin can thus carry a person into an exciting new world of spiritual discoveries.

Thus I urge you to seek a *tough repentance*. The Christian life is not an easy way out—not by a long shot. But why take the easy way anyhow? Life is by nature a challenge. We should truly enjoy the rough path of a consistent holiness as we gradually become more like the Messiah. Look beneath the sin to the real issue. Seek a total change, no matter how difficult—a change of the heart. Seek a total reorientation to *God's* way.

If it requires the hard work of Bible study, prayer, confession of sins, planned actions, and even humiliation, go ahead and submit to the God who is able to completely deliver you. Do not consider yourself a weakling. You are not so fragile that you will break under difficult conditions.

No matter how much defeat you have found in your life, you are not incapable of doing the difficult when it comes to repentance. You must *expect* yourself to be strong! Remember that you are not doing it alone. Remember God. Children of God do not need to be afraid of the darkness of tribulation or the challenge of repentance. Children of God have a spirit of power, love, and self-discipline (2 Timothy 1:7). Not a single one of us is exempt from the challenge of this growth process. None of us is perfect—*we all need to change!* But we all have access to the power necessary for change.

Although your feelings may tell you that you are not strong or capable, the truth of Scripture tells you otherwise. Therefore, if your feelings say that you are weak, then you will have to use your mind, based on the truth of Scripture, and oppose your feelings. Our faith in the Lord is not so much a faith of feelings as *a faith of truth*. When truth and feelings disagree, truth must be the light that guides us, for it is the truth that sets us free, even free in our thoughts and emotions (John 8:32).

When you consider repentance, remember that in and of yourself you can do nothing. So although you have a major part to play in the changing of the orientation and perception of your life, you must recognize that God will take the greatest responsibility. Repentance involves your reliance on God to work in your life. It is *God* who is right when you and God disagree, so rely on him. Then you will live by the truth, rather than by your own ignorant bliss. Repentance is a decision to more completely follow Jesus Christ and to thankfully accept that he will then carry you most of the way down the path of your life.

But even though God travels with you on your way, the forces of evil are lurking along the path, waiting to trip you in order to put you out of action. But take heart! If you stand up to the devil, he will run away (James 4:7). Think of it as rolling up your sleeves and taking on Satan in the power of the Holy Spirit. But remember that you are going out into battle with God—God is not tagging along with you. It is in *his* power that you will have victory.

To attempt to deal with Satan by our own power and reasoning is foolish (1 Peter 5:8-9, Jude 9). Even before man's nature was corrupted by sin, Satan was more powerful and intelligent than man. So we must lean heavily upon our relationship with God and the strength he provides through the Holy Spirit's ministry in our lives. We must wear the entire armor of God in order to both defend and attack in our daily spiritual battles (Ephesians 6:10-18).

Vulnerable on Either Side
Man can be a very high or a very low being—a child of God or a child of darkness. Our strengths and weaknesses can be used righteously or unrighteously. We sometimes exercise the option to use our God-implanted attributes in ways degrading to other human beings. We can indeed use our own personal resources

toward very negative ends. But this kind of improper use of our abilities goes against the grain of our calling as Christians. We have crossed over from death to life (John 5:24). However, the forces of darkness are still at work even after we are joined to Christ.

For those of us who belong to God's kingdom through faith in Christ's death and resurrection, Satan battles not for our destiny, but for our will. He wants the children of God to act as children of darkness, leading unholy lives rather than doing God's will. In the midst of our battle, Satan tempts us to use our God-given strengths in sinful ways. However, at the same time God is asking us to use our strengths for his work in this hurting world. If we realize that our strengths can be used either sinfully or righteously and that we are in the midst of a spiritual battle, we should determine to use our strengths as weapons for the side of good, for we are on God's side.

Some of our strengths are like wild horses that need to be tamed. As I mentioned before, I used to be a wild horse of a Christian with an anger which needed to be tamed. Realizing that my anger could react wildly again, I need to keep it under control, making sure it is used only for God's purposes. I must keep in mind that my anger is like a bronco, with no domestic heritage. While it is one of my greatest strengths, it could nevertheless be used wildly in the world of sin.

You may have a personal strength which you generally use in a righteous fashion, but which could also be used to exploit other people. Look at this strength from God's perspective. Don't measure yourself against others who have this same strength, but consider your abilities in light of God's particular plan for your life (Galatians 6:4-5). It is often in the areas where you are strong that you will be tempted to judge others in their weakness.

Beware: Satan wants to use your strengths to *his* advantage. So when you are tempted to gloat in your strength or to use it for a sinful purpose, remember that no temptation is irresistible (1 Corinthians 10:12-13). God wants you to ride out upon the *tamed* horse of your strengths in order to wage an earnest battle against the dragons of sin.

Your personal, God-given weaknesses can also be used in a sinful way. When you think less of yourself because you are unable to do things God does not even want you to do, that is sin. Destroying your positive self-image by focusing on your inability is a blow struck against the cause of righteousness. If you begin to feel worthless about yourself, remember that *God explicitly created you to do certain righteous works in this world.* For you to try and try and try to accomplish things which have not been assigned to you by God and for which you are not equipped is a tragic sin.

Indeed, you are vulnerable in both your strengths and your weaknesses. But take heart! There's no need to raise a white flag of surrender. Victory is ours in the Lord! Not only do you have certain strengths to use in your ongoing battle against sin, but you have the power of our Commander in Chief with you. For God has a personal interest in your battle.

But the options are still yours: you have all the spiritual potential at your command—all the weapons and power you need. This is step six—to fight against your own sin. It is basically your decision whether you will be a hero or a deserter on the spiritual battlefield of your life. Decide this day whether you will serve boldly in the army of God. It can make all the difference in your self-respect.

Work sheet instructions for: "My Battle Against Personal Sins"

The Left Column ("Sins Which Hold Back My Self-Respect")
In the left-hand column, list the sins in your life that hold back your godly self-respect. These are the large sins in your life. Certainly all sins hold you back from respecting yourself, but some hold you back more than others—these are the big sins you need to do

something about right away. It's those repetitive sins which really hamper our walk with God and our service to him. Put a *check mark* in each of the little boxes in this column only after you have confessed the particular sin to God and made a resolution with him and with yourself to wage a full-scale battle against that sin. Be sure that you fight these especially difficult sins with the strength of the Lord—"in his mighty power" (Ephesians 5:10). You cannot be victorious on your own.

The Middle Column ("Others Who Can Help Me")

In the middle column, list Christians who can minister to you in your battle to overcome the sins listed on the left. As we have said before, God does not expect us to have victory in the Christian walk as independent Christians. To be a total maverick is to be an unsuccessful Christian, since it is not God's will. Therefore, try to think of people who could understand and maturely handle your confession of the sins you've written down in the left column.

These may be close friends or they may be people who have openly admitted their own struggles with the same sins you are dealing with; perhaps they have *overcome* those sins in their lives. List all the people you can approach to pray for you, counsel you, hold you accountable, and call you up every so often to see how it's going.

The people you list need to be people you can trust. It is preferable that these be people who can admit their own sins and keep everything confidential. It's very difficult to go to people who act as if they're perfect. Often self-righteous people, who rarely expose their weaknesses or sins, make us feel unacceptable, and thus we avoid going to them to expose our own weak areas. Now this doesn't mean you shouldn't go to *confident* people. Confident people who can admit that they blow it from time to time are usually the most helpful people of all. They have confidently dealt with personal sin, but they do not pretend to have reached some great state of spiritual perfection.

The Right Column ("My Plans to Attack These Sins")
In the right-hand column, either after you have completed the other two columns or as you deal with each sin independently, write down a brief plan of action. Later you can develop it into a fuller, more complete plan of action. Your strategy may be to avoid the kind of situation which brings the temptation to commit a particular sin. This may entail learning to think a different way about your sinful behavior. Or you might plan to study some Scripture regarding the particular sin you have listed. This is the time to plan to contact a certain person in order to sit down, confess your sin, and pray together.

Plans to deal with sins in your life can be very diverse, so be creative. Always remember to pray for God's power that your study of Scripture will instruct you concerning how to deal with life, so that you will know how to avoid each particular sin. Furthermore, put some feet to your prayers and your Bible study by planning some sort of action which you would consider to be a course of valiant battle. James 4:7 tells us, "Resist the devil, and he will flee from you." Do battle with your personal sin. Approach this third column with Christian courage. Trust in the Lord's deliverance through the power of the Holy Spirit.

My Battle Against Personal Sins

Sins Which Hold Back My Self-Respect	Others Who Can Help Me	My Plans to Attack These Sins
Count yourselves dead to sin but alive to God in Christ Jesus. Therefore do not let sin reign in your mortal body so that you obey its evil desires. (Romans 6:11-12)	Confess your sins to each other and pray for each other so that you may be healed. The prayer of a righteous man is powerful and effective. (James 5:16)	Because he himself [Jesus Christ] suffered when he was tempted, he is able to help those who are being tempted. (Hebrews 2:18)

☐ _____

☐ _____

☐ _____

☐ _____

☐ _____

☐ _____

_____

Work sheet instructions for: "The Sin Potential of My Strengths"

This second work sheet recognizes that almost all our gifts from God can be misused. Our personal characteristics, desires, abilities, and talents can all be used in sinful ways.

If one of your abilities is to talk openly with others, then you should use it for the Lord. But if you use that ability to get close to people solely for the purpose of selling them a bill of goods, that would be sin. Your *motivation* usually distinguishes whether or not something is a sin.

Perhaps one of your strengths is your ability to study the Bible in depth. That's quite a strength, and it can be very helpful to you and to others. But suppose that you were to decide to use that strength to show other people that you are better or more spiritual than they are. To use it for personal recognition or gain would be a sin. In this case, you would write down in the left-hand column, "Ability to study the Bible in depth," and in the right-hand column, "For personal recognition or for making someone feel negative about himself."

If you are able to recognize that your strengths can be used unrighteously or sinfully, then you will be much more apt to keep them under control. Your strengths are like wild horses to be tamed and used for others. While they are untamed, they will be used for *self* at the expense of others. For this reason you need to list the sin potential of your strengths so that you will be aware of them and able to keep them in check.

The Sin Potential of My Strengths

Strengths   **Ways of Using These Strengths Unrighteously**

_____

_____

_____

_____

_____

_____

_____

_____

_____

_____

_____

_____

_____

_____

_____

_____

_____

_____

_____

Work sheet instructions for: "The Sin Potential of My Weaknesses"

Complete this work sheet on weaknesses as you did the second work sheet on strengths.

The Sin Potential of My Weaknesses

Weaknesses   **Ways of Using These Weaknesses Unrighteously**

_____

_____

_____

_____

_____

_____

_____

_____

_____

_____

_____

_____

_____

_____

_____

_____

_____

12

STEP SEVEN: PUTTING THE SOUL INTO ACTION

Stand firm. Let nothing move you. Always give yourselves fully to the work of the Lord, because you know that your labor in the Lord is not in vain.
1 Corinthians 15:58

What is true spiritual growth? What good is the Christian way of living—with its godly self-identity, devotional life, strengths, weaknesses, sanctification, and battle against personal sin—*if* you do it all hiding within the shelter of your own life? What practical value is *your* life beyond your own doorstep?

The seventh step brings us to the threshold—we look out upon the world in all of its complexity, suffering, and challenges, and we wonder: *what part of the world is for us?* Which challenges are specifically ours? What suffering are we perhaps called to go through in the process? Although a kind of infinity exists out there in the world, God has chosen a certain, special, finite portion for each one of us.

The Mirror Which Sends Us Into Action
No Christian should be able to look at himself in the mirror of his born-again identity and feel a godly self-respect *if* he is not serving in the work of the Lord. For if, amid his idleness, he is convinced that he has a godly self-respect, he has probably succeeded in fool-

ing himself. You can apply steps one through six in your life and still not have a complete self-respect. For as long as you do not put your faith into action, you have simply undergone a kind of spiritual hypnosis.

A counterfeit self-respect and a life of spiritual inertia cannot bring much satisfaction to an individual. A Christian should respect his lifestyle only when his God-given abilities are employed in the common life and work of the church (the church gathered) and in ministry to the secular, humanistic world (the church dispersed).

Why focus on the importance of *action*? Let's find our answer by taking a look at the greatest event in all human history: the sacrificial death and victorious resurrection of Jesus Christ! Because God himself has saved us from eternal death and given us eternal life, we should be totally enraptured with and committed to our heavenly Benefactor—*if* indeed we truly believe as we say we do.

Life has infinitely more meaning when we give of ourselves to God, rather than constantly taking more and more from him. God designed us and saved us for the purpose of serving him by spreading his love to a dying world. Thus our lives should be God-centered, God-motivated, and God-obedient.

Brothers and sisters in the Lord, it is time to stop putting top priority on our own agendas and to start getting in touch with God's agenda for our planet. He has much he wants to do in society—there are so many to love! He wants us to be *in the action!* Our powerful God wants a powerful church! But Satan, as in the Garden of Eden, continually tries to sidetrack us from God's battle plan by enticing us to focus on our own needs, wants, and desires. Listen—we don't really want to cooperate with the enemy, do we?

Our very responsible God will supply our needs, reduce our wants, and change our desires if we simply center our attention on him. He will never expect so much of us that we will miss what is most important for our lives. We need to trust the Lord to provide for us and then leave our individual striving behind us.

We should be truly inspired to love God as an expression of gratitude for his profoundly beautiful gift of the Messiah. Since we are his children—children of the light—let us move into even the dark corners of the world in the power of God to do his good work. "For we are God's workmanship, created in Christ Jesus to do good works, which God prepared in advance for us to do" (Ephesians 2:10).

Jesus tells his disciples that their faith will move them to live in service as he did. In fact he says that his followers ("anyone who has faith in me") will accomplish even greater things than he did (John 14:12). We were designed to take part in meaningful ministries, to reach out and do things we have never before imagined possible. Such great ministries are achievable only because he works now through us, the people of God. What an excellent honor! May we truly handle it as such in our lives!

Each One a Minister

We must remember that we each have a particular piece of the action. For we have all been called to serve, administering God's grace to many. The Lord has designed everyone in the church to have a significant place of service. Since all the parts of God's intricate plan for his people are in some sense interdependent, no part is superfluous or expendable.

It should not be possible to talk of one individual's ministry apart from the larger whole. Therefore, each piece of the Master's work is critically important, and each of our parts in the great drama of life is equally essential. Small parts are as indispensable and critical as all the others.

Francis Schaeffer expressed this concept quite well in his book *No Little People* (Downers Grove, Illinois: InterVarsity Press, 1974, p. 18): "As there are no little people in God's sight, so there are no little places. To be wholly committed to God in the place where God wants him—this is the creature glorified." Because all people and all tasks are important in God's plan, we can be content in the place and responsibility he has assigned to us. In fact, such contentment is a prerequisite for *additional* responsibilities (Luke 14:7-11). There are no *greener* pastures—all green is from God's hand. One place of God-assigned ministry is as good as any other.

By this point in our discussion, you have probably done some serious thinking about yourself. Hopefully you have come face-to-face with the fact that God has designed you for ministry. If you still have negative feelings about yourself, then you are probably struggling with the material you've read. Good! Keep struggling! Deliverance is worth the effort. As you are reforged by God for his service, you will inevitably come to see who you really are—according to *his* determination.

Perhaps this is all very difficult for you because you are still telling yourself that you are not worthwhile or capable. If this is the case, take some time to review the first six steps. Meditate on 1 Corinthians 3:5 ("The Lord has assigned to each his task") and 2 Corinthians 3:5 ("Our competence comes from God"). Memorize 2 Corinthians 3:18. And talk to a good friend and to God about your negative self-image.

Going Outside the Camp
Before we examine how you can find your primary ministries, let's take a look at some of the responsibilities which apply to all Christians. We are all called to witness in our daily lives to God's salvation in Jesus Christ. (However, we are not all called to a ministry of evangelistic efforts such as missionary work, revival, etc.) Similarly, we are all called to do the "one anothers" of Scripture, for it is through mutual ministry that we build *one another* up for the work of the church.

Most of God's will for our lives is actually spelled out clearly in the teachings of Scripture, where God clearly points out the agenda of our daily walk with him. God is even more interested in our constant relationship with him than he is in our major ministries. But if our relationship with God is solid, then we will naturally want to serve him in the most significant way we can. That is one reason why our *final* step is the pursuit of God-appointed ministries.

Obedience to the teachings of Scripture will automatically and circumstantially bring us to many daily ministries. We need to have a sense of readiness and willingness to serve, unlike the priest and the Levite who passed the wounded man on the road from Jerusalem to Jericho without giving aid (Luke 10:25-37). While they had certain major responsibilities in religious ceremonies, they did not take the time to serve God along the road of their lives.

As servants of God, we are sometimes called to soil our lives when the needs of others match our abilities. Jesus shows *us*, in the parable of the good Samaritan, that we need to be flexible in our service. Even though lending aid would have made the priest and the Levite ceremonially unclean, thus eliminating them for a while from their major assignments, God still expected them to help the wounded man. These important, unforeseen ministries which have a sense of urgency about them have priority. Continual obedience to God's on-the-spot instructions takes at least ninety percent of our time.

A word of caution: it is likely that your major assignments from God may take you outside the safety of Christian fellowship. Jesus was crucified on an infamous executioner's hill, surrounded by two thieves and a cursing mob. "And so Jesus also suffered outside the city gate to make the people holy through his own blood. Let us, then, go to him outside the camp, bearing the disgrace he bore. For here we do not have an enduring city, but we are looking for the city that is to come" (Hebrews 13:12-14).

Keep in mind that your ministry assignments come from God. They may or may not be some of the standard church jobs (church school teacher, usher, hospitality chairwoman, etc.). Comparison of your strengths with your opportunities may lead you outside the church building—"outside the camp"—to ministries such as neighborhood visitation, social involvement, or jail counseling, to

name just a few. But such ministries should call forth as much commitment and preparation as teaching Sunday school. Going outside the camp means risk, and so it calls for dedication.

Something Just for You

There are two basic means by which you can learn what major
ministries God is calling you to: your knowledge of God and your
knowledge of yourself. We all realize that God is unique. You, too,
are unique—consider your personal qualities and your life circumstances.

We learn about God's ways and character in the pages of the
Bible. Then in our unique walk with the Lord, he reveals himself
and his will. Jesus tells us the direct, relevant truth when he says,
"Whoever has my commands and obeys them, he is the one who
loves me. He who loves me will be loved by my Father, and I too
will love him and show myself to him" (John 14:21).

If we cannot be trusted to obey God in the daily, common
assignments given to us all, then why should God trust us with
larger, more specific ministries? We can detect this very logic in
the parabolic message of Jesus: "'Well done, my good servant!' his
master replied. 'Because you have been trustworthy in a very small
matter, take charge of ten cities.' . . . [His master] replied, 'I tell you
that to everyone who has, more will be given, but as for the one
who has nothing, even what he has will be taken away'" (Luke
19:17, 26).

It is critically important for us to actively pursue God's truth
through serious Bible study. For then we will be able to think as
God thinks and to put *his* ways into our lifestyles—his ways of
handling life and helping people. Only then will a reciprocal love
flow between each of us and Jesus Christ.

In that intimate love affair, marked by our joyful obedience,
Jesus promises to reveal himself to each one of us individually. In
whatever manner that may occur—by new understanding from
Scripture or by spontaneous thoughts of Jesus prompted by the

Holy Spirit residing in us—the Lord will communicate to us further knowledge of our assigned ministries, including at least one major, ongoing task.

Jesus will certainly let us know his concerns. He does not hide the pressing matters of his mind and soul. "Jesus called his disciples to him and said, 'I have compassion for these people; they ... have nothing to eat'" (Matthew 15:32). The Lord still shares his concerns with *us*, his new disciples.

As we develop a loving relationship with him, Jesus lays a specific burden of compassion on our hearts and points us to specific ministries. At first we might find his special assignments almost unachievable, with the same kind of incredulity as his early disciples, who said, "Where could we get enough bread in this remote place to feed such a crowd?" (Matthew 15:33). But eventually Jesus will show us how he intends to use us effectively in his work.

The First Six Steps: A Stairway of Confidence
The previous six steps for building your godly self-respect can be extremely helpful as you attempt to perceive God's ministry assignments for you in this seventh step. In a very meaningful way, God has masterfully implanted his announcement of your ministry assignments in your very creation. Your personality, your strengths, and your weaknesses all say something about God's will concerning your service to him.

As you continue to ponder the truth of *step one*, "Custom-Designed by God," you should feel progressively more special through the years, more and more like God's person with a purpose, a quest to fulfill. The wonderful reality of Psalm 139:13-16, Jeremiah 1:5, and Ephesians 2:10 can give you the kind of secure self-image, anchored in God, which is necessary to be able to commit yourself to whatever service God asks of you.

As you become victorious in *step two*, "Walking Free With the Architect," you will find in your walk with God a freedom to be yourself, to perceive the world from your own unique, God-given perspective, and to think your own creative thoughts. You will appreciate your own personality as fashioned by the Creator, and you will come out of hiding by opening channels of communication to heaven through your prayer, Bible study, and obedience to God. The Lord will accordingly bless the lives of many people as they observe your unique walk with him.

As you get in touch with your strengths in *step three*, "Strong Enough to Serve," you will find that God's tools for your ministries are revealed. Since God designed you with particular ministries in mind, you ought to be able to discover God's specific callings to service when external circumstances and opportunities call for those very strengths God has placed in you. Thus you will see open doors for service all along the intricate pathways of your life. Both small and large tasks which require your predominant strengths can be adopted as personal short-term and long-term ministries. As the truth of step three brings you to further maturity in your life, you will find a special kind of self-acceptance as you see how God has marvelously equipped you.

Step four, "The Advantage of Weaknesses," can release you from self-degradation, freeing you from depression and worry. You will have more energy to consider obedience when you stop misinterpreting your weaknesses. As you thankfully accept your innate weaknesses as qualities designed for you by God himself, you will begin to taste the freedom not to have to do certain things. The confining and demanding bars of unrealistic expectations in the communal life of the church will fall as people reach out to help each other in areas of weakness.

Your weaknesses help you to recognize those certain areas in which you have not been called to serve God, except perhaps in emergency situations when someone with the truly appropriate strengths is not available. When you accept your inabilities as God-designed, you will detour away from the danger and disappointment of wrong ministries—the right work being done by the wrong person. You will thankfully accept that many attractive tasks are given to others that have not been given to you. You will also learn to recognize that many mundane tasks need to be done—by yourself *and* by others. The freedom not to have to succeed at every spiritual work will transform your life!

Step five, "Refined in the Fire of Life," can take you through a unique dimension of spiritual growth. Life is inevitably seasoned with spiritual trials for each of us. Through all the anguish and exhilaration of the growth process, you will gain an important maturity and wisdom which will enable you to discern your God-designed ministries. God is very adept at recycling the junk in our lives—all the negative past experiences we tend to keep buried inside. Sanctification—our spiritual development through the process of the Holy Spirit's guidance—prepares us with a perseverance which is essential in ministry.

In *step six*, "Declaring War on Your Sins," you can learn to grow through your dedicated battle against your own sins. But it's not really like fighting against yourself. You are fighting *for God*. The self-denial required by the battle will open your heart to God's mind.

In the battle against your sins, you must let go of your selfishness, and in those moments of untainted perception you will recognize the needs of others. The needs you recognize as you escape the tunnel vision of serving your *self* might just be an indicator of a ministry just for you. As you develop a warrior's stand toward sin, you will fight difficult battles and flex spiritual muscles you didn't even know you had. Hopefully you will come out of each battle stronger and more courageous for God's service.

The Last Step Is With a Real Foot
The seventh step is like a seventh trumpet, signaling the active pursuit of ministries you can call your own. *Step seven*, "Putting Your Soul Into Action," is the bottom line for a steadily growing godly self-respect. Without the implementation of this step in your life,

you are at best no more than a wageless, unemployed servant in the kingdom of God, and at worst a pitiful egoist.

Step seven is a call to *action*. Heed the words of Scripture: "Do not merely listen to the word, and so deceive yourselves. Do what it says" (James 1:22). Don't make the Bible into a philosophical word game. *Do* what you know you should do!

What indeed is true Christianity? What is the most convincing demonstration of the real thing? Look again at Scripture: "Who then is the faithful and wise servant, whom the master has put in charge of the servants in his household to give them their food at the proper time? It will be good for that servant whose master finds him doing so when he returns" (Matthew 24:45-46).

It is vitally important to do God's work, not to merely fool yourself into believing that you are doing his work. Consider Jesus' description of the fate of such pretenders: "Not everyone who says to me, 'Lord, Lord,' will enter the kingdom of heaven, but only he who does the will of my Father who is in heaven. Many will say to me on that day, 'Lord, Lord, did we not prophesy in your name, and in your name drive out demons and perform many miracles?' Then I will tell them plainly, 'I never knew you. Away from me, you evildoers!' " (Matthew 7:21-23).

Locating God's perfect spot for you in his plan is very important. You will respect yourself much more when you are doing what God wants you to do, at the place where he wants you to do it. But in order to get there, you'll have to move not only your mind, but your feet as well.

I meet so many people who are focused hopelessly on themselves. All they can talk about is their plans, their accomplishments, and their goals *ad nauseam*. Then they spend their lives worrying about self-enhancement and self-actualization and other "self" nonsense. And do you know what? They never arrive. Beyond every self-centered dream is yet another dream, and usually a trap.

Oh, that we might adopt the selfless attitude of knights in the

King's army: we would diligently train for spiritual battle, and only after we had fought the good fight would we return to safety. We would then be able to feel satisfaction that the necessary *action* had been taken and we could be satisfied that the kingdom was resolutely advancing.

The Path of Service Has Already Been Blazed

A careful study of the Scriptures gives overwhelming evidence that our self-respect is to be based on service to the Lord. The Old Testament contains example after example of godly individuals doing what God called them to do. From Noah's courageous ark-building all the way to the prophet Malachi's warnings to Israel, person after person is spoken of in light of whether or not they were obedient to what God wanted them to do. The spiritual trail has in a sense been blazed for us by those who have acted in resolute faith. In many cases just one obedient act in the life of a true believer gained him or her biblical recognition.

Consider the prostitute Rahab, who simply hid a few spies who were from the army of Joshua. She is greatly acclaimed in Scripture as a faithful, obedient servant of the Lord (Joshua 2 and Hebrews 11:31). James said of Rahab and her act of courageous obedience, "Was not even Rahab the prostitute considered righteous for what she did when she gave lodging to the spies and sent them off in a different direction? As the body without the spirit is dead, so faith without deeds is dead" (James 2:25-26). There it is, spelled out in biblical black and white: God wants our faith to be accompanied by action. When we know that this is his desire, how can we have self-respect if we are not actively involved in his work?

In the New Testament we're told of the eternal God who became a man in order to live among us and show us a righteous human lifestyle. In those four marvelous gospels by Matthew, Mark, Luke, and John, we see over and over again that when God the Son walked on this same planet we walk on, he wore the cloak of *service* to those who were hurting and seeking to be rescued.

God expects us to serve him. Paul repeatedly relates God's concern for our partnership in his work:

> Stand firm. Let nothing move you. Always give yourselves fully to the work of the Lord, because you know that your labor in the Lord is not in vain. (1 Corinthians 15:58)

> For we are God's workmanship, created in Christ Jesus to do good works, which God prepared in advance for us to do. (Ephesians 2:10)

> Be devoted to one another in brotherly love. Honor one another above yourselves. Never be lacking in zeal, but keep your spiritual fervor, serving the Lord. (Romans 12:10-11)

We will have the right kind of joy and self-respect only when it sinks into our minds and souls that we are not here for the narrow pursuit of self-service. Then we will no longer strain our muscles to pat our own backs. In the midst of our own dedication, we will hear the Master say, "Well done, good and faithful servant" (Matthew 25:21).

Our Father, The King

In your pursuit of personal ministries, it is important to adopt a firm identity as *God's child*, in whom he delights and through whom he plans to share his goodness. It is therefore imperative that your identity not be grounded in lesser callings. Your primary sense of selfhood should be established in your spiritual sonship.

Many times people get caught up in their vocations or in material things, such as cars, houses, and recreational pursuits. But in all of this, your status as a child of the King and your God-appointed ministries should be foremost in your mind as you consider who you are. Then, as a true son or daughter of the King, you will expect meaningful, godly pursuits from yourself.

Because you have the security of knowing you are a King's child, you do not have to worry about tomorrow's trials. You will have full assurance that you and God together will not fail. Instead, you will confidently live out your ministry and calling in each day's opportunities.

But perhaps you feel that you don't have the right attitude to go out and seek God's appointed ministries for your life. You want to serve the Lord with a light and joyous heart but you are not yet there. The good news—news for which we are accountable—is that God desires an obedient heart even more than he desires a joyful spirit.

Consider again Jesus' parable of the two sons (Matthew 21:28-32). Jesus was being questioned by Jewish priests and elders who had worked all their lives to be pious, holding up toward God their sacrifice of allegedly good intentions. In this parable, Jesus was pointing out that God is pleased with those who do his work despite their initially poor attitude. But God, on the other hand, is *not* pleased with those who say they are going to serve him, but who do not follow up their promise with action.

God is calling to you, summoning you to find your appropriate ministry and get to work. But the work will not follow until you have the right attitude. Your challenge is to be like the son in the parable who changed his attitude, doing at last what his father desired.

Let us not be the kind of son or daughter who sweetly promises to go, but who never shows up when people are in need. All of us in the church are needed for God's work. Each one of us is called to walk a certain path as a distributor of God's goodness to his creation.

After the church gathers together for strengthening, it is simply to be sent back out again. We are to be at work salting the world—in office buildings, factories, neighborhoods, hospitals, carpentry shops, and really anywhere at all. For *everywhere* there are people in need of the touch of God.

The assignments God gives you will often look like more than you can handle. That is to be expected, since those assignments are never for you alone. For God always includes *himself* in your projects for him. And he usually assigns more than one person to each project.

As God makes resources available to you, including companions in your ministry, you will have good reason to be confident. For God has seen to it that you are qualified for whatever he asks of you. Keep in mind the encouragement of God's word: "Do not throw away your confidence; it will be richly rewarded. You need to persevere so that when you have done the will of God, you will receive what he has promised. . . . We are not of those who shrink back and are destroyed, but of those who believe and are saved" (Hebrews 10:35-36, 39).

Why be discouraged? Everything works out well in the kingdom of God *if* we do things God's way. We have this in our favor: our Father is the King.

> Though an army besiege me,
>   my heart will not fear;
> Though war break out against me,
>   even then will I be confident. (Psalm 27:3)

A Caterpillar—Not Yet a Butterfly

For one reason or another, many of us have wanted to hold a great variety of jobs in the church. However, we need to always keep in focus that God has created each of us with a different cluster of abilities, personality characteristics, life circumstances, and values. Your own unique combination makes you just right for a particular type of ministry.

As you continually become more effective in that one area of service—like a skilled woodworker who keeps getting better and better—you can gain a sense of excellence and personal joy which should not be abandoned merely to try out other areas of ministry. In this sense, variety is not necessarily the spice of life.

After you become committed to a certain ministry, stay with it, unless God calls you to another ministry or to your eternal home. Now perhaps God is calling you to more than one major ministry. That's great! But don't try to find your variety just by trying a ministry here and a ministry there. God will supply enough variety for you in the various people and circumstances you encounter in those assignments which are undeniably from him.

Stay on course. The caterpillar stage precedes the butterfly stage. Don't be too quick to flit around like a butterfly from ministry to ministry, but make the steady, direct progress of the caterpillar. In the church we seem to have too many would-be jacks-of-all-trades and too few experts—too many butterflies and not enough caterpillars.

A spiritual skill is a valuable thing. Hence, if you are well-equipped by God to teach Sunday school, why not let your church leadership know you are available for at least the next few years? Make the godly commitment of talent *and* time.

You are not a mere optional worker in the church. You have already been hired—by the Big Boss. You are in fact a critical part of some vital ministry necessary for a strong body, necessary for the work of some church in your community, whether the people there know it or not. It is true—God has already called *you*. He has called you to put your soul into action.

On our own we are nothing—but with God we are something! We have good reason to be confident. He created us in his image, and, although we have fallen away from him, he is re-creating us back into his image through the gracious mediation of our noble Savior. But this is not a passive process. We, the children of God, are called to *actively* serve our Father in his work.

If you recognize the imprint of God's signet upon your life, then you will gain the motivation to serve. *Only after you find yourself can you give yourself.* This is what Christian service is all about; this is the reality each of us is called to *live*. So live it! Take the steps necessary, whether seven or seventy, to grow within. *Grow in your self-identity.* Growing *inside* empowers and inspires us to serve *outside*. In this way, the body of Christ will be healthy enough to storm the gates of hell until the time when we enter the gates of heaven.

Work sheet instructions for: "My Pursuit of God-Appointed Ministries"

The Left Column ("Ministry Opportunities")
In the left-hand column, list various opportunities for ministry which come to your mind. These could be church jobs or other potential assignments the Lord may be leading you to consider (for example, a neighborhood Bible study moderator). I would encourage you to list some of the jobs available in your church. Don't worry if they are filled—list the ministries most appealing to you (a possible signal of God's leading), whether they are filled or vacant.

After you have listed several jobs down the left side, analyze each of them to discover God's leading concerning ministries for you. By filling in numbers across the page, you will arrive at a score for each of the items from this left-hand column. The score which is highest would appear to be the ministry for which you are best equipped. Those ministries in which you tally considerably fewer points are those for which you are probably not well equipped.

Column One ("I Am Already Able")
As you score each ministry opportunity, give yourself a score of either 0, 1, or 2 points, depending on your present ability to perform that particular ministry. If you've done it before and you know that you do it well, give yourself a 2. If you've done it before, or something similar, and you believe you can do it but you're not quite certain, give yourself 1 point. If you have tried that kind of thing before, or something similar, and have definitely not been able to do it, give yourself a zero. If you have never tried it, give yourself a zero.

Column Two ("God-Given Personality Traits")

As you think through each of the ministries you listed, consider what kinds of personality traits would go well with each task. For example, if the task you are evaluating involves a lot of public speaking and you are a shy person, you might give yourself a zero. If, when you turn to the subsection "My God-Molded Personality Traits" of your work sheet entitled "My God-Redeemable Life Experiences" (at the end of Chapter Ten), you find words you have listed there that seem to be the character traits of a person who is able to stand up and speak publicly, then you might give yourself a 2. If you feel you are somewhere in between, give yourself 1 point.

Column Three ("The Deeper Desires of My Heart")

This item relates to exercises one and two of the work sheet entitled "My God-Inspired Desires" at the end of Chapter Ten. If the ministry you are rating is related to your answers to at least one of those questions, give yourself 1 point. If not, then give yourself a zero.

Column Four ("My Past Experiences")

For a ministry or task, assign 1 point if you feel that your past has given you a unique understanding of and a special sensitivity to the work of that ministry. This is a different focus than that of the first column, which asks if you are able to do it. In this particular case it is your life experiences rather than actual ability that might give you an "edge" in doing the tasks of the ministry you are rating and evaluating.

For example, if you have taught adult Sunday school before and this is the ministry you are rating, then look carefully at the subject matter of the class you will teach. If you have raised a number of children successfully and they are following the Lord, then you could put a 1 in this column if the class is on Christian parenting. But if the class is on God's will and you have struggled with that over the years, put down a zero.

Column Five ("In the Realm of My Spiritual Gift")
This item focuses on the spiritual fact that you are a channel for
God's mighty power. If the subject of spiritual gifts is unfamiliar to
you, seek counsel from an experienced Christian friend or your
pastor. Basic Bible passages dealing with spiritual gifts are
Romans 12 and 1 Corinthians 12.

Give yourself 3 points if you have a spiritual gift that relates to
the ministry being evaluated. If you know that God's power is not
working through you when you do the kinds of things called for in
the ministry you are rating, give yourself a zero. If you are not quite
sure, give yourself a 1 or 2, according to your own judgment.

If you are totally unfamiliar with this subject of spiritual gifts,
leave this column blank. It will not greatly affect the results of this
work sheet.

Column Six ("The Burdens of My Heart")
This item relates to exercises three, four, and five of the work sheet
entitled "My God-Inspired Desires" at the end of Chapter Ten. If
the ministry you are rating is related to your answers to at least one
of those questions, give yourself 1 point; if not, give yourself a zero.

Column Seven ("I Am Likely to Sin")
This question requires a "yes" or "no" answer. If you answer it
"yes," give yourself *minus* 14 points. If "no," give yourself 2 points.
Notice that if you give yourself minus 14 points, you will be unable
to score *any* points on that particular ministry. If you would have
otherwise received a fairly high score, you will have all the more
motivation to eliminate that sin in your life. For it would appear
that God has designed you to function in that particular ministry.
Therefore, do battle against those sins that would hold you back.

We all sin. The issue here is whether or not you are sinning or
would be likely to sin in key areas of ministry. Prayerfully consider
this matter, and if you are still confused, seek advice from your
pastor or from a close Christian friend.

Column Eight ("My Favorite Bible Passages")
This question does not ask you to minimize the importance of any parts of Scripture. But every one of us has a few favorite Bible passages that speak to some issues which we feel are very important. Give yourself 2 points if one of your ten most favorite passages deals with the focus of the ministry you are rating. Give yourself 1 point if one of your next ten favorite passages speaks to the content of the ministry. If none of your twenty most favorite passages relates to the ministry you are rating, give yourself a zero.

Column Nine ("If I Had Only Five Years to Live")
This item relates to exercise two of the work sheet entitled "My God-Inspired Desires" at the end of Chapter Ten. If the ministry you are rating is one of your answers to that second question, give yourself 1 point; if not, give yourself a zero.

Column Ten ("Other Factors")
In this column, write in whatever special factors you consider to have been left out of this work sheet study. Assign one point.

Column Eleven ("Total Points")
Total all scores across horizontally for each ministry opportunity and compare scores, seeking God's leading.

Note to class leader:
Have each class member relate the results of his work sheet. Use extra time to have the group help anyone who did not come up with a predominant ministry or any high scores. If someone did not know of available or possible areas of service or had any other problems with the work sheet, then take some time to work out the problems. Furthermore, the class members should pray for each other's developing ministries.

If the group is composed entirely of members of the same church, you might want to make a list (after acquiring each individual's approval) of the primary ministries of all the class members, and then possibly pass this list on to your pastor or someone else in your church leadership. Remember that the success of your work with this group ultimately lies in each member's active pursuit of his or her God-appointed ministries. Therefore, follow-up with church leadership might be helpful.

My Pursuit of God-Appointed Ministries

Ministry Opportunities	1 I Am Already Able	2 God-Given Personality Traits	3 The Deeper Desires of My Heart	4 My Past Experiences	5 In the Realm of My Spiritual Gift	6 The Burdens of My Heart	7 I Am Likely to Sin	8 My Favorite Bible Passages	9 If I Had Only Five Years to Live	10 Other Factors (write out)	11 Total Points
	2	2	1	1	3	1	-14	2	1	1	